# Going Postal

# Going Postal

### Willie R. Hargis

ARPress
ILLUMINATING IDEAS.
EMPOWERING VOICES

**ARPress**
45 Dan Road Suite 5
Canton, MA 02021

Hotline:        1(888) 821-0229
Fax:            1(508) 545-7580

Ordering Information:
Quantity sales. Special discounts are available on quantity purchases by corporations, associations, and others. For details, contact the publisher at the address above.

Printed in the United States of America.

ISBN-13:        Softcover       979-8-89356-034-3
                eBook           979-8-89356-035-0

Library of Congress Control Number: 2024902946

# Table of Contents

# Introduction

This book reflects the thirty-two years I served as a postal employee and a couple significant years prior to my postal career. Many points of interest and experiences in my life formed the person I have become, and this book tells how those points in life affected my postal career and ultimately me. A factor that significantly contributed to this adventurous journey was the time I spent in the military. Beginning with that, this series of short stories will take a close-up look at those experiences, and the stories will also address how those experiences affected my life—and why I went "postal."

# Chapter 1

## Queers and Steers

After I received notice that I was being drafted into the US Army, three close friends and my then girlfriend threw me a going-away party. The last thing I recall of that night is lying on the floor and someone pouring beer in my face. Somehow, I got to my girlfriend's house and passed out on her couch with her by my side. It was a pleasant surprise the next morning to wake up and see this lovely person lying next to me. I looked at my watch and realized I did not have much time prior to reporting to the departure site. So I did what I had to do, and afterward I jumped in my car and drove from Los Angeles to Compton as fast as I could. After arriving in Compton, I did not have time to shower or do any kind of personal hygiene, so I got my parents to drive me to my departure location in downtown LA for my new adventure. I reported to the site on May 5, 1965, and from there I flew to Fort Polk, Louisiana, for basic training, with one stop in Phoenix, Arizona. That was a significant stop that I will address later.

After arriving at Fort Polk and reporting to the induction station, where I believe we were sworn in and given other instructions, I noticed some of other the guys there. I know I must have lit up the place, smelling of beer that was soaked into my clothes from the night before, as well as other smells on my body that were probably not pleasant to those around me unless they were in a like condition. I do not remember anything of significance other than the fact I was now in the army and that I was with others who probably had similar concerns and focuses.

We were issued gear and took a bus ride to the barracks to which we were assigned. We got off the busâ€"or truck, I do not recallâ€"and hit the ground running. My life was in for a big change from that point forward.

After arriving at our barracks, we were under the guidance of the infamous Sergeant Barge, whom I will never forget. Sergeant Barge was a drill sergeant extraordinaire. He was a gangly, slender, but apparently tough and tough-minded person. He had a unique way of expressing himself, at least different from anyone I had known up to that point, and his varied expressions served to entertain me, as well as motivate me. Experiencing Sergeant Barge and his uniqueness turned basic training into an interesting time and helped the process go by quicker.

On my first day at Fort Polk, and more specifically the first evening, we had our first group meeting in the barracks. After we had gone through the formalities of induction and settled in for the evening, we had a group introductory period. Prior to the meeting, all kinds of saying and clichés were spouted about. Even though I was born and raised in Texas, one of the clichés resonated with me, mainly because I was living in the Compton area of Los Angeles, California, when drafted. I overheard someone in the group say that only queers and steers came from California. Since I was a born Texan, that comment did not concern me, at least not until the evening of our introductions to one another. Sergeant Barge went around the room asking everyone to introduce themselves to the group and to give some detailed information about their background. Part of that introduction included our place of residency.

To place the following information in perspective, I must go back to events of the days prior to the introductory meeting. On the night before I was to report to the army, my friends gave me a going-away party in South Central Los Angeles. The next morning, I rushed home, smelling like a keg of beer and with no time to shower and got whatever I was required to take with me. My parents took me to the induction station.

Now, this became significant in what took place my first night in the barracks and during the introduction period. My family was very close-knit, and my parents were always there for me. Surely there was nothing wrong with their accompanying me to the induction station—or so I thought. Unknown to me at the time, some inductees at the induction station had noticed me being accompanied by my parents. I was probably one of very few, if not the only, of the inductees who had parents tagging along to the induction station, who by the way also walked with me to the point of no return. I am sure many of the inductees had their girlfriends, friends, or possibly their wives sending them off to war, but not me—the mama's boy. The Vietnam conflict was hot and heavy at the time, and I was going into a life with many unknowns, so my parents hugged me and said their goodbyes before I went off to war. Now, back to the night in question. When the time came to introduce myself, I was a little nervous and my voice cracked when I tried to speak. My voice went a few octaves higher than normal, and I had to clear my throat to get it back to normal. That event set the stage for future events.

When my voice cracked, I heard laughter as my voice emulated one not thought of as a man's voice. From that point forward, I had to defend my manhood and deal with those guys who had seen me at the induction station with my parents in tow. These fellows were from some of the toughest neighborhoods in the Los Angeles area, including Watts. No one called me gay or anything of the sort, but there was an underlying feeling that I might be gay, which led to my being repeatedly challenged.

Several occurrences helped me get beyond the gay perception, though. Part of an individual's introduction to the army consisted of providing information about one's background, including schooling and work accomplishments. In high school, I had the privilege of ascending to the position of colonel of our National Defense Cadet Corps (NDCC). (The segregated school systems of the South, and more specifically, the schools of Fort Worth, Texas, did not have the privilege of having ROTC programs in their schools. Therefore, our city's Black schools had the NDCC program, but unlike the ROTC program at White schools, Black cadets were required to purchase their own uniforms.) As colonel of the Dunbar High School National Defense Cadet Corps, I gained military training that afforded me an advantage over my fellow basic trainees. In addition, prior to reporting to the army, I had worked at a company where I supervised about fifteen people. The army recognized my leadership background as a former supervisor and as an officer in the NDCC. Based on these and other accomplishments, Sergeant Barge selected me as one of four acting platoon (guides) sergeants for Company B, Third Battalion.

Imagine a kid from Fort Worth, Texas, being in charge of soldiers from all over the United States, including White soldiers from the South and those tough brothers from Watts, California. I had my work cut out for me—and that "soft" stigma to overcome.

Despite Sergeant Barge's recognition, some soldiers in my unit still thought I was a little soft, if not gay. However, that perception changed when we went to our physical training events. I was athletic and very quick with my hands and feet. When we performed agility drills, I was always near the top if not at the top in performance. On one day early in basic training, we did an exercise in which we fought with pugil sticks, an event that showed everyone what kind of man each person really was. One trainee by the name of Porras, who got on the plane in Phoenix, Arizona, did not appear to me at first to be an impressive physical specimen or as strong as he later proved to be. He just looked fat to me, but he was by far the toughest soldier in the heavyweight group. He stood about five feet, ten inches but probably weighed well over two hundred pounds. He was a fighting machine and whipped all comers.

I was a member of a lighter weight group whose average weight was around one hundred sixty pounds. I weighed about one hundred fifty pounds soaking wet, but I was the best and possibly the toughest in my group. With my quickness, I was able to defeat all my opponents by beating them to the punch. After that exercise, I gained respect from almost all in our barracks. I also participated in boxing events, displaying that same speed of hand in putting up good fights even with those who had several pounds on me, which gained me more respect. I finally got those first few days behind me.

As acting platoon guide, I functioned as the platoon leader, and those under my guidance were required to follow my instructions. One day I ordered one of the White trainees to do push-ups after he failed to complete drill instructions correctly. The trainee did not like my order and told me that he was going to kick my ass after we completed basic training. However, when training was over, he shook my hand and never mentioned the incident.

Another incident early in basic training probably set me apart and established how I would continue to deal with life's challenges. I have never considered myself highly intelligent, but it seemed that I was always seeing the big picture, which set me apart from the other soldiers. As part of our physical conditioning training, we ran in the hot June sun in Louisiana, making for nearly one hundred degrees every day. On the day in question, the mess sergeant requested volunteers to perform kitchen police (KP) duties. I quickly volunteered. Everyone thought I was crazy and wondered why I was volunteering for KP duty, as we had all heard how tough it was supposed to be. I could not imagine anything tougher than running in the hot Louisiana sun, so I eagerly volunteered. I even received a compliment from the mess sergeant, who told me that I had a great attitude and, if I did not change, I would go places. I chuckled to myself, knowing that my intentions were to get out of the hot sun, not necessarily to display any traits I may or may not have had. In fact, to prove my decision was an excellent one, I sat outside in the shade, peeling potatoes, as I watched my unit run by. I was as happy as any soldier in basic training could be, taking all things into consideration. In addition, while on KP, I was able to eat and drink all I wanted. What a great move. I felt I had outsmarted the other trainees and was beginning to define myself.

Early in basic training, Sergeant Barge and the other drill sergeants set out to change our behavior. One thing Sergeant Barge and the other sergeants set out to change was how we approached mealtime. On the first full day of basic training, we went to the mess hall and, as we would do at home, sat down and took our time enjoying our meal. However, after a couple of bites, Sergeant Barge and the other drill sergeants came into the mess hall and ordered everybody out. Most of us had very little to eat. The message was to get in there, gulp that food down, and get out. The next time we went to the mess hall, we took care of business. I still have the habit of eating too fast to this day. Things calmed down a bit so that we did not have to eat in as much of a hurry, but we had learned not to kill a lot of time in the mess hall.

One fun thing I recall about the mess hall was the milk machine. Growing up in a relatively poor family, we had no extras. We had the necessities but no luxuries. I soon realized that once I went into that mess hall, I could drink all the milk I wanted. I would enter the mess hall, stop in front of the milk machines, and drink no fewer than two glasses of chocolate milk and one or two glasses of white milk before filling up the glass with white milk one more time before sitting down to eat. I thought I was really living large.

One other important point in relation to the mess hall was the food the army served. Even though early in training I had one of the largest steaks that I had ever eaten, the steak meal was not the one I most remembered. Most soldiers have fun memories of SOS, the army's version of hash beef and gravy on toast, or as we called it, shit on shingles. SOS was the breakfast meal served in the mess hall more often than any others and a meal I initially hated but learned to love.

Because I was a young Black man without many good examples of men in leadership positions, Sergeant Barge was an inspiration and a role model for me. We developed a good working relationship. In selecting me to be one of his platoon guide sergeants, a position that was awarded largely based on a soldier's background, Sergeant Barge placed me in direct competition with the other platoon guides in our company. In that I was the only Black platoon guide in Company B, it appeared to me that, at least part of the time, Sergeant Barge was harder on me than he was on the other platoon guides. So one day, after experiencing what I thought was disparate treatment, I questioned Sergeant Barge about it. I told him that it appeared to me that he was not as tough on the White platoon guides as he was on me. Sergeant Barge kindly explained to me, as an older Black male to a younger Black male, that he wanted me to be the best, and by pushing me harder and demanding more of me, I would be better than the others. That was all he had to say. I worked harder and tried to separate myself from the other platoon guides.

Based on my continued effort to stand out, midway through basic training, Sergeant Barge recommended me for a competition. He selected me to compete against other soldiers in our battalion for special recognition as the top basic trainee. Those of us chosen competed in drill procedures and were questioned on our knowledge of military terms and procedures. I did well but did not win the competition. I made a mistake in the rifle-drill portion of the competition and was unable to answer one question in the interview portion. I was asked about the Latin term esprit de corps, which means "spirit of the unit"—I was not familiar with it.

Sergeant Barge was a witty person as well and always used sayings that just cracked me up. One evening I asked Sergeant Barge whether he had a girlfriend, and you would have to have been in the military to understand and appreciate the humor in his answer. He proceeded to tell me that he indeed had a girlfriend and asked me if I had not seen her. I told him that I had not. Sergeant Barge went on to describe his girlfriend and stated that she had breasts as large as two butt cans and that she had an ass as wide as two wall lockers. The butt cans he referenced were half-gallon vegetable cans filled with water and placed on the supporting beams in the barracks for soldiers to place their cigarette butts. The wall locker was where we kept our clothes and was about two feet wide. That exchange was very funny to me, especially as a young trainee who had not seen many women while in basic training and could only imagine what he was describing.

On another day while going through drill procedures another unforgettable event took place. One of the trainees with whom I had developed a friendship and just happened to be one of those tough guys from Watts was having problems with drill procedures. After turning in the wrong direction on several commands, Sergeant Barge became fed up with him and directed him to report front and center, at the front of the group. When he did, Sergeant Barge went asked him some very pointed questions. At first, we did not know where Sergeant Barge was going with his questions, but in a short time it became very clear.

He asked the trainee, and I quote, "Soldier, if a mama pig and a daddy pig had a baby, what would it be?"

The trainee answered, "A baby pig, Sergeant." Sergeant Barge then asked, "If a fucked-up mother and a fucked-up father had a baby, what would it be, soldier?"

The trainee paused for a minute and, with a strange look on his face, answered, "I don't play that, Sergeant."

The entire group almost died laughing even though we were somewhat concerned about this tough guy's reaction to our laughing at him or the question. He was embarrassed but did not mention that incident further.

That was one of the funniest exchanges I had encountered during basic training, although there were many more. On other occasions, Sergeant Barge would challenge our fitness during running exercises. He would tell us that he and Sergeant Johnson, his drinking partner, had been out all night long drinking whiskey, and while running beside us, he questioned why we could not keep up. He even invited us to smell his breath to verify his story. Sergeant Barge was truly a gem and a person I will never forget.

Drill sergeants used certain terms in basic training that still intrigue me to this day. Here are a few examples: inside man, outside; outside man, inside; upstairs man, downstairs; downstairs man, upstairs; and front and center, to name a few. When I spout these sayings today, those who did not have the privilege of attending basic army training think I have lost it. In addition, as we ran almost everywhere, we sang cadence, which took our minds off running. Sergeant Barge would sing cadence as we ran, and one of his favorites went like this, "I have a girl who lives on a hill. She won't do it, but her sister will. Sound off, sound off, sound off, one, two, three, four." I got pretty good at singing cadence for the group, and early one morning as we were running, we came across a young lady wearing a red dress and standing next to a soldier right off the road. We had previously sung a cadence that went like this: "See that girl dressed in red. She makes a living in the bed. Sound off, sound off, sound off, one, two, three, four." Well, you guessed it, as soon as we got in front of the young lady, I took my turn singing cadence and let it fly. We got a great laugh out of the incident.

We did not have many extracurricular activities other than drinking 3.2 beer (beer with 3.2 percent alcohol content) in the evening after we completed training, especially on the weekends. One evening we went to the post's movie theater to see Goldfinger, a James Bond movie. We lined up outside the theater waiting on the doors to open, and while we waited in line, people allowed their friends who were just arriving to get in front of them. The problem seemed to be happening more with the Black soldiers, and the White soldiers took exception. They started pushing in the line, which started swaying back and forth. I believe we came very close to having a few fights break out, but the MPs showed up and restored order.

After several weeks of training, we were given a break and allowed to have a little rest and recuperation. We left Fort Polk and headed down to Lake Charles, Louisiana. Lake Charles had this one long street in the city where Black soldiers were welcome and where both good and bad activities went on. However, several White soldiers who hung out with Blacks accompanied us there. A friend of mine from Las Vegas named Terry Johnson had interests similar to mine, so we decided that we would not go to the red-light district part of the street to pick up girls; instead, we wanted to go to the more respectable end of the street where the American Legion was located and where the so-called good girls went to meet soldiers. Terry and I were of the opinion that we would do just as well with the girls at the American Legion club as the other soldiers would do with the prostitutes on the other end of the street.

On the way down to the American Legion, we stopped and bought a small bottle of liquor. We walked into the dance area as if we were a couple of fellows who knew our way around with the ladies. We proceeded to talk to some of the more attractive girls and got a couple of them to come over to our table. The two young women drank our liquor and left us sitting alone at the table. Well, we surmised that meant so much for trying to charm them into going back to our hotel room. We proceeded to walk toward the other end of the street, not sure what if anything we could get into, especially since it had gotten late in the evening. As I approached the red-light district, I saw a group of soldiers, some of my friends from Company B, standing around this one attractive woman, begging her to go with them. I stood there for a few minutes and then made a very bold move, unlike any I had ever made before. It was likely based on the evening's earlier frustrations at the American Legion or the combination of that and the whiskey I had consumed while visiting with the other young women. I walked up into the middle of the group of soldiers who were surrounding the young woman, grabbed her by the hand, and walked out with her. That move made up for the wasted time at the other end of the street. The R&R was over. After breakfast the next morning, we headed back to Fort Polk.

On our way back, we stopped in a little town outside the post called Leesville. A group of us went into a little juke joint to have a beer. A young woman was sitting over to the side counting money. Stupid me walked up to her and asked if she had had a good night. She looked up at me and said, "Did I f--- you last night?"

I replied no, and she said, "Well, I did not have a good night."

I did not take this as a compliment, mainly because her choice words made all the fellows laugh at me, not her.

We were soon back at Fort Polk and finishing up our basic training. An event was about to take place that would demonstrate my leadership ability and how much respect I had gained from some of those who had initially questioned my manhood or toughness.

Before going into that, I would like to give a little background information about how I, as well as my brother, was influenced to take the step I was about to take. As a youth growing up in Fort Worth, my brother and I had the privilege of meeting one of top local disc jockeys. This man was proud of the fact that he was an army paratrooper. He used to brag to us about being a Screaming Eagle, of the 101st Airborne Unit. We were both impressed, but I never considered being a paratrooper. However, my brother decided to become one, and I then I became interested. My brother knew I was thinking about volunteering to become a paratrooper and decided to write me a letter in which he asked me to talk to him prior to joining up. I wanted to join and had every intention of talking to him before volunteering. However, a special guest come to our unit to attempt to recruit us to become paratroopers, and he made a very appealing presentation. He was a recruiter from an airborne unit; stood about five feet, eight inches tall; and was in his dress uniform. He looked great with his sergeant strips, medals, ropes, and citations. I am not sure if we noticed that he had bloused boots or knew the significance of them, but what we saw thoroughly impressed us. For the record, only paratroopers can place the hems of their pants into the top of the boots, which is called bloused boots. In his presentation, the recruiter said something to the group that changed my life, probably established me as a leader, and further distanced me from that first impression that some in the group might have had of me. After wrapping up his pitch, he stated, "If you have to call home to ask your mama if you can become a paratrooper, we don't want you." At that time, I remembered what my brother had told me. I had every intention of calling him first, but I had to demonstrate that I was a man and did not need to talk to anyone prior to making the decision I was faced with. The sergeant's routine worked on me. As I got up and stepped forward to volunteer, one of my friends from Los Angeles asked me if I was joining. I told him I was, he got up with me, and the whole group followed us. I was now a true leader and had gained full respect of my guys. We had our final physical and mental test to see how much we had learned and how far we had come physically. If we scored high on both tests, we would be promoted to E-2, which came with an opportunity to be selected to go to the advanced leadership school prior to attending advanced infantry training. I did very well on both my physical and mental examinations. In the physical part of the training, several events had tested our physical fitness, such as the run dodge and jump, parallel bars, grenade throw, low crawl, and mile run. I did well in all the events except for the low crawl. I had injured my wrist when I was in my early teens, which affected its strength. The weakened wrist caused me to have trouble crawling fast and keeping my upper body off the ground. But in the end, I scored 487 out of a possible 500 points in the physical portion of my final test, which put me in the top 5 percent. However, there was a problem in how my mental examination was graded. I did not find the written test difficult, so after seeing my low score, I began wondering what had happened. In examining the test paper, I realized that the instructor had graded my test incorrectly. When calculating my score, he failed to add points from the second page to the final score, which only reflected my score from the first page. Even that by itself, though, was a passing score with just over seventy. But on the whole test, I scored over ninety. The incorrect score was enough to pass but prevented me from receiving other benefits from the high score. I spoke with my sergeant about the mistake, and he set up a meeting for me with the company commander. However, by that time, the grades had become official, and it was too late to correct. My commanding officer offered to write a letter of recommendation for me to my next duty station, which he did, but I was not in the group that received a promotion to E-2 and was therefore not eligible to participate in the class for advanced leadership training. But I had a letter in my file that did not hurt my efforts. Basic training was over, and I had proven, at least to some, that there was no question about my manhood, toughness, persuasiveness, or leadership abilities in an all-male environment. I also became aware that I could compete with anybody—white, Black Hispanic, or anyone else.

As a reward for completing basic training, we were allowed to go home for a short period. However, prior to packing up, I got a pleasant surprise. My brother, who had just completed a mission to the Dominican Republic, came down to Fort Polk and spent the last day with me. I was so proud of him. He showed up wearing his Special Forces paratrooper uniform, complete with silver wings on his chest, a green beret on his head, and spit-shinned, bloused boots that only paratroopers could wear.

So that you can appreciate what all the trainees there were seeing I will need to explain. Except for the recruiter who visited us, we saw only drill sergeants and officers on post. We did not have the privilege of seeing any bloused-boots-wearing paratroopers, and we surely did not see anyone wearing a green beret or in the Special Forces, which at the time was the elite of the elite. As previously mentioned, only paratroopers could wear their pants bloused into their boots, and only soldiers in the Special Forces could wear the coveted green beret, or any beret at that time. Most of us had heard about the Green Berets, but none had seen one in person. I had my chest stuck out a mile as if I were the one wearing the Special Forces uniform and the green beret. I think that everyone who saw my brother was just as proud as I was—well, except for one officer in our unit. It was obvious that he did not appreciate the presence of this soldier all dressed up in his Special Forces garb. After seeing my brother in the area, he required everyone to snap to attention, including my brother. He began to be especially tough on the rest of us as we were trying to finish our job cleaning the barracks for the last time and getting our things ready to depart Fort Polk. After seeing my brother there, my decision to become a paratrooper was reinforced.

At last, I was on my way home. At that time, home was not the Los Angeles area, where I had entered the army, but my birthplace, Fort Worth, Texas. While I was at Fort Polk, my parents had taken a trip to Texas and then moved there after I completed basic training. Therefore, my brother and I traveled to Fort Worth to visit them rather than back to LA. After a great stay, it was time to report to my next duty station.

# Chapter 2

## Here We Go Again

My next duty station was Fort Gordon, Georgia, where I was scheduled to take Advanced Infantry Training, (AIT). However, my trip to Fort Gordon required a stopover in Atlanta. I boarded an airplane in Fort Worth, bound for Atlanta, and to my surprise a classmate of mine, Emmett Johnson, was on the same plane. We had gone to school together at Dunbar High School in Fort Worth, and he had completed basic training at Fort Polk as I did. After arriving in Atlanta, we had a four-hour layover at the Atlanta bus station, so we just camped out, waiting on the four hours to pass. While we were just killing time, a White man approached us and started a conversation. We were somewhat suspicious of him, particularly because he was White, and we were not accustomed to having White men being friendly to us for no reason, especially in the Deep South. He offered to show us a good time while we were in Atlanta. Well, that invitation brought on more suspicion about his intentions, but being young and stupid—for the lack of a better explanation—we agreed to go with him. We also figured that if he started any trouble, we were more than able to take care of ourselves.

We struck out on foot, heading to the alleged fun place. We walked about twenty blocks from the bus station to a part of town that appeared to be predominately Black. We went into an establishment that at first glance appeared to be just a small eatery, and as we entered, I realized it was just that. I thought, Why did this man bring us to this place? As we walked through the building and to the rear, we crossed over to another section that appeared to be a nightclub. Well, not only was it a nightclub, but it was loaded with women as well. At that time, Emmett and I thought this White guy was really an all-right person and that we were lucky he had approached us.

Shortly after we entered, an older woman approached me and started a conversation. She began telling me about her son, who was also in military service. She told me that, because her son was in the service, she wanted to be nice to other soldiers. Yeah, right, I thought. Later, as I was talking to another woman, I looked in the mirror on the wall across the table from me, where I was able to see the people in the club as they were walking by. As I was watching, something clicked inside me; I had a feeling that something was not right. The more I observed the people walking by, the more uncomfortable I became. The reason suddenly became apparent to me: the people I was observing in the mirror were not women but men, all dressed up like women or in drag. What I had been observing was men impersonating women. At that time in my life, I was unaware of this practice and didn't even know that gay bars existed. But a closer look around the room confirmed what I thought I was seeing. I looked over to see where the White man who had brought us to the place was, and I located him with one of the impersonators. They seemed to be having a great time. He had obviously already known what I was just realizing. The situation called for some quick decision-making—I had to come up with a plan to get us out. I leaned over and shared my concerns with Emmett, who was hugged up with one of the impersonators. He looked around as if to question my conclusion, but the look on his face confirmed that he agreed with me. I whispered to him that we needed to get out there. I suggested that, in order not to attract undue attention, we should not leave at the same time. I suggested, as you probably figured, that I leave first and that he should wait a few minutes before following me out. He agreed. I got up, unassumingly walked toward the exit, and then got the scare of my life. Standing in and partially blocking the doorway was a six-foot-tall female impersonator. I knew I had to get out of there, so I sucked it up and continued to walk toward the exit. When I got to the door, my fears came to reality. The large impersonator grabbed my arm, which scared the crap out of me, and asked, "Are you coming back?" I nodded my head and said yes. I eased by him and walked gingerly through the eatery, not wanting to appear to be in too big a hurry, and then I went out front door. I waited a few minutes for Emmett, which seemed like a lifetime, and when he finally walked out the door, the two of us ran all the way back to the bus station. That was truly a scary series of events and a lesson well learned about seeking adventure and trusting strangers. I was glad none of those guys who initially wondered about my manhood had seen me in that place. I would have had to prove myself all over again.

We waited at the bus station, and started to laugh about the whole experience. Not long after we returned to the station, our bus arrived and we proceeded to Fort Gordon. The rest of the trip was uneventful—as was the ensuing training.

Shortly after we reported to Fort Gordon, and prior to beginning our training, the sergeants presented us with an opportunity to give. They asked us to donate to a local orphanage. Being a son of the South, the first thing that came to my mind was whether this orphanage was integrated or not. Was I being asked to donate to a White orphanage? Since I was in Georgia, it did not take me long to figure that one out. I asked the sergeants for more information, but that did not go over well. I do not recall what the sergeant specifically said in reply, but I am sure he called me something like a smart ass. Regardless, I knew I would not be donating to a segregated orphanage.

My group was assigned to training to fire a recoilless rifle mounted on the back of a jeep. The rifle was really a canon that was called a tank killer. We were told that if we fired the recoilless rifle at a tank and missed, we had to vacate quickly because the tank could easily locate the jeep and strike, which was not survivable. We were also schooled in making and delivering Molotov cocktails, which involved easing up next a tank and throwing the improvised bomb inside. The recoilless rifle was fun to fire, and each time, it would lift the jeep up off the ground. We also received training in firing a .50-caliber machine gun, which was a beautiful piece of machinery and very powerful. The .50-caliber was said to be able to penetrate the armor of a tank.

Advanced Infantry Training was new and exciting as well as physically demanding. We did not have much time to think about evening activities because, when we completed our day of training, we just wanted to shower and go to sleep. However, it seemed we had more evening time, and we entertained ourselves with different activities, including shooting dice.

During the period I was in training at Fort Gordon, my brother was stationed at Fort Bragg, North Carolina. We communicated with each other, and one day he called and asked me to accompany him to New York City to visit some friends. I could not legally travel that far from my post while on weekend leave, but I was going to take a chance anyway. I had just received my monthly pay and had enough money to buy a round-trip bus ticket, but I did not have enough spending money. However, I had another way to raise what I needed. I had been somewhat lucky with dice in the games we played, so I entered a game in hopes of getting the additional money. Ultimately, I did quite well. I won more money than I needed for the trip. However, while in the process of cleaning out the guys I was playing with, the barracks came under siege. Drill sergeants raided our barracks after receiving information about possible gambling. I just happened to be in the upstairs section of the barracks and was able to put away the dice and the money before the sergeants got to our area. Initially, that series of events went in my favor. I had won all this money, and the game had ended because of the raid, right? Not so fast.

One of the soldiers I was shooting dice with was Emmett Johnson, my old schoolmate. I had taken all his money except for his last five dollars. After the raid, he started begging me to give him a chance to win some of his money back. I told him no because of the possibility of being caught and getting in trouble like the others. He continued to pester me, and I soon gave in. He only had five dollars left, so how long would it take me to relieve him of that? Most have heard the old saying, "Follow your first mind." I had learned that in elementary school, but on that evening, I failed to heed the good advice. As you have probably figured out, Emmett won his money back, all the money that I had won from the other soldiers, and some of my own money, as well.

I was in a dilemma. What will I do about the trip to New York City? I still had enough to buy a ticket, but I would be broke for the rest of the month. I chose not to take the trip. I called my brother and informed him of my plight. I instead took a trip back to Atlanta for my R&R weekend.

There, I did something that I did not believe I would. I returned to the "scene of the crime" just to see if the eatery was still there. It was, but it was closed. I was not planning to go in again, but I was curious about the place. I had told the soldiers I was traveling with about my experience, and they also wanted to see if it was still there. No one—at least, no one I had met—knew gay clubs existed. My story was something of groundbreaking news to most I shared it with in 1965.

To graduate from AIT, we were required to complete certain physical tests, including doing ninety deep-knee bends within a specified period, running a sub-six-minute mile, and completing a certain number of push-ups and six chin-ups within a specified period. If someone did not complete the physical tests, that person could not go on to Jump School. I was able to pass each physical test, but I had difficulties doing the required chin-ups. Some may surmise that doing six chin-ups should be a simple endeavor; however, I had injured my wrist as a child, and my right wrist was not very strong. I did five chin-ups very quickly, but due to either psychological or physical limitations, I had a difficult time getting my head above the bar for the sixth time. Ultimately, I did, and I was on my way.

After passing all the required tests, Advanced Infantry Training concluded. Those of us who had signed up to be paratroopers boarded a bus and got on our way to Fort Benning, Georgia. We were a bunch of crazy soldiers riding through small towns in Georgia. In one small town, I think everybody on the left side of the bus saw the same thing that I did and at the same time. A young woman of a lighter persuasion was sitting on the front porch of her house, and she had her dress up above her knees, with her legs gaped wide open. Now you know what happened next. Everyone on the left side of the bus, especially the brothers, called out, "Whoooo!. That was an uplifting sight for a bunch of sex-starved soldiers. If you do not understand that, let us move on.

We stopped at a church on the way and had dinner. I was accustomed to eating with the White soldiers while we were on a military post, but all my experiences off post were under segregated circumstances. However, a new day was dawning. It did feel very strange to eat in an integrated setting somewhere in Georgia, of all places, in 1965 without being on a military post.

# Chapter 3

## Going Airborne

We soon arrived at Fort Benning to begin our three weeks of airborne training, called Jump School. Life as I had previously known it was about to change. Becoming a paratrooper would be one of the most challenging endeavors I had ever taken on in my life. I did not have a clue about what I was about to go through. I soon learned what my brother had evidently wanted to talk to me about.

After getting off the bus from Fort Gordon, we literally hit the ground running. I quickly learned that there was no such thing as walking at Fort Benning. You had to run every place you went, including the mess hall. In addition, the drill sergeants put us under more scrutiny and dealt out more punishment for making mistakes. It appeared that everybody was being required to do additional push-ups for the smallest of mistakes. After seeing what was happening to the other trainees and all the other things that were going on, it became necessary for me to become invisible—a tactic I had learned as a teenager when my then girlfriend asked me to take her to a party in the Lake Como section of Fort Worth, which was on the wrong side of town for me, where she had once lived and was going to school. I did not want to go, but I could not let her think I was afraid. I was, but I also knew I had to man up. I knew that to become invisible, I could not bring any attention to myself. To be invisible, I did not dance or move around; I stayed in one spot. I left a little early, before the party ended, which was strategic. Usually if there was going to be trouble, it would occur at the end of the party. Nothing happened, meaning that my strategy had worked. I thought that was smart on my part.

Well, to become invisible at Fort Benning, I could not make any mistakes or bring any undue attention to myself. I saw soldiers targeted by the drill sergeants based on their failure to follow precise instructions, stupidly challenging authority, or displaying an attitude upon receiving instructions. Some soldiers were required to do additional push-ups or other physical tasks, while other soldiers busted out of Jump School based on their attitude or failure to adjust. During Basic and Advance Infantry Training, the drill sergeants rode us hard, and if any failed their training, they could be recycled and have to go through the training again—but they did not bust out. Not so in Jump School. Only the right type of soldier could wear the wings of a paratrooper.

Over the next three weeks, I successfully became invisible and was not required to do any additional push-ups or other exercises for making mistakes. In the process, with just the normal physical training, I became the fittest I had been in my life.

Jump School consisted of three grueling weeks of physical exertion. On top of running everywhere they went, trainees were required, it seemed, to participate in an all-day physical exercise program to make them physically fit. Part of the process used at Jump School was to weed out the weaklings, those with bad attitudes, nonconformists, and those who could not keep up with the rigid pace required by the drill sergeants. I saw many acquaintances fall by the wayside for the above reasons and fail to become paratroopers.

The three-week training course was broken down into three segments. The first week consisted of jumping off platforms that were about ten feet of the ground to perfect landing techniques. We were also required to jump out of simulated airplanes. This exercise required the trainee to have a dummy parachute with a static line attached to it, which was then attached to a guideline. As we jumped out of this simulated airplane, we slid down the guideline. The slack in the static line created the feeling of free falling, which was like jumping out of a real airplane.

The training was very intense, and I was too serious about what I was doing to allow myself to enjoy the experience. However, I took notice of one soldier who, as he ran back to the simulated airplane after each jump, had a smile on his face and seemed to be enjoying the exercise. Every time he made his jump, he would yell out "Airborne!" with emphasis on air. His antics got me excited, and I began viewing the exercise differently. I started to enjoy myself a little, despite the grueling circumstances.

Because we were about twenty feet off the ground when we jumped out of the simulated airplane, the exercise did have a slight fear factor. I eventually came to see the jump like a scary amusement-park ride or roller-coaster and started enjoying it.

The second week at Fort Benning was Tower Week. When we first entered the campus, one of the first things we saw was the two gigantic towers, which were approximately twenty stories tall. Only those who were lucky saw the purpose of the towers. They were part of paratrooper training. The exercise involved a soldier strapping on a harness, being raised to the top of the tower, and then dropping from the tower in a parachute. To be more specific, the soldier would put on the harness of an opened parachute attached to the tower apparatus. This apparatus would raise the parachute several hundred feet in the air, and the parachute would separate from the apparatus. The soldier would then float to the ground as if he had jumped from an airplane. We were all looking forward to Tower Week and to falling from those huge towers. Well, not really. It did appear to be a very scary exercise—scarier than any amusement-park ride. As it turned out, we did not have to participate in Tower Week due to rain that week. We were so disappointed that we could not fall from the tower (tongue in cheek). Instead, we continued with week-one exercises to perfect our jumping and landing skills, which were needed when jumping from a real airplane.

In the third week of Jump School, called Jump Week, required us to jump out of a perfectly good flying airplane. This was a highly anticipated time, as we would place into practice all we had learned and that was drilled into us over the previous weeks of training. This was also the time, as that old saying goes, when the boys would be separated from the men.

I must mention a ritual that some soldiers practiced prior to jumping from a plane. Several soldiers went to church the night before their first jump. I attended church as a youngster, but I had not gone for several years and chose not to go with the others. My rationale was that I did not want to burden God with a selfish prayer that night when I had not done the right thing for years and had failed to worship him as I should have. I felt it would have been hypocritical of me to go to church at that time.

Back to the upcoming event. Jump Week included our first trip to the airfield, where we boarded a live Air Force C-130 cargo plane. After boarding the C-130, we all sat down with our parachutes strapped to our backs. As the plane took off, we sat there with our eyes wide open, and nary a word was spoken. As we flew to the drop zone, better known as the DZ—basically a cleared area with no trees—we sat there anticipating the jumpmaster's order to get ready, which we all knew was coming next. After that order, we stood up and attached our rip cords to the static line. Our hearts were beating a thousand miles an hour as we anticipated when the green light would come on, indicating it was time to jump. As the pilot approached the DZ, we encountered a problem. At the front of the line was an officer who was making his first jump, as we were, but he had been in a different training program. Strangely enough, this officer did what we called "froze in the door." He was first in the line and, subsequently, was required to be the first one to jump. The pilot had only a few minutes to fly over the DZ, so all the prospective paratroopers had to jump out during that short time. The jumpmaster, who was normally a sergeant, had the responsibility of ensuring that all of us got out of the plane while we were over the DZ. When the green light came on and the jumpmaster yelled, "Go!" he quickly realized that the first person in the jump line was stuck, just standing in the door, not moving. What happened next provided me a clear understanding of what group of soldiers ran the army. The jumpmaster put his foot right on the officer's behind and literally kicked him out of the airplane. Most of us, especially since this was our first jump, were scared to death, as was the officer, and we might have frozen in the door as he had done had it not been for what we had just observed. After seeing the size of the Jump Master's boot and watching him "help" the officer make up his mind to jump, the rest of us had no problem deciding to jump when we got to the door.

That first jump was truly magical. After the initial blast of the wind in my face as I jumped and after the parachute finally opened after a few seconds of free falling, the float down to the ground was just the greatest feeling I had ever experienced. Later I would tell all who would listen that jumping out of an airplane was the second-best feeling in the world. To the best of my recollection, we made three jumps that week, which was a requirement to graduate from Jump School. I do not recall much of the second jump, but the events of the third jump I will never forget. For two distinct reasons, those memories are burned into my memory. The first thing that went wrong on that jump was that I failed to do something I had been instructed and drilled on numerous times: to secure the parachute's harness that wrapped around my upper leg. As I got into the harness, I did not get it tight enough to keep it from sliding around my lower body. The harness had to be tight around my legs for a very specific reason. However, it was not tight enough, and my testicles were between my leg and the harnesses strap. This caused pain that kept me from concentrating on the things I should have been concentrating on. Most of the trip down, I was trying to adjust the harness to relieve the pressure on my testicles. I was successful, but I lost track of what I was supposed to do prior to landing. In the first two weeks of training, we were instructed over and over to bend our knees slightly to lessen the impact of hitting the ground. When I finished fooling around with that harness, I thought I had my knees slightly bent, but I soon realized that they were bent about halfway up. I would have seriously injured myself if I had landed with my knees in that position. However, right before hitting the ground, I went through a mental checklist and quickly realized that my knees were not in the right position for landing. As soon as I finished adjusting my legs and positioned my knees correctly, I immediately hit the ground. Was I lucky or just blessed with a guardian angel?

I had completed everything required to graduate Jump School. The graduation ceremony involved those enviable silver wings being placed upon my chest. That was a proud moment for me and for my friends who started out with me in basic training. We had accomplished something only a select few soldiers had the privilege of accomplishing. We were officially Army Airborne Paratroopers and could distinguish ourselves from other soldiers by blousing our boots. The next step was the assignment to our permanent units. When we had started the journey back in basic, we all figured we would end up in Vietnam. As fate would have it, there were other plans for my group and for me.

During the second week of Jump School, after we had completed our training for the day, we were sitting around one afternoon discussing where we would likely go after Jump School. One of the older soldiers in our group, who was a sergeant, told us that if we did not want to go to Vietnam, we should join the Special Forces. We initially thought he did not know what he was talking about and was out of his mind. Anybody who knew anything about the Special Forces, especially during the period in question, knew that Special Forces soldiers trained specifically for Vietnam. Once we challenged the sergeant, he explained his rationale: if we were accepted into the Special Forces, the training would be so extensive that, once completed, a draftee who had to serve only two years in the army would have less than a year remaining to serve. He went on to inform us that the army would not send a soldier with less than a year to serve to Vietnam. This was intriguing to me for two reasons. As I mentioned earlier, my brother was in the Special Forces, and he was stationed at Fort Bragg, the home of the Special Forces and of the Special Warfare School. Being reunited with my brother would be a dream come true. The second reason I was interested was that I wanted to wear that coveted Green Beret.

Previously, the criteria for becoming a Special Forces soldier included being what is called a triple volunteer. A candidate had to volunteer for the army, which consisted of a three-year commitment at that time; volunteer to be a paratrooper; and last, volunteer for the Special Forces. Due to the Vietnam conflict and the depletion of the Special Forces ranks at Bragg, the Special Forces was for the first time allowing draftees to join and attempt to qualify for the Special Forces in two of their schools that did not require training that was as extensive and time-consuming as the other disciplines. Some classmates and I found out where the testing was taking place and went. I was fortunate to pass the test required to enter Radio Operator School. Unfortunately, I was the only one of my group from basic training, except for one White guy from Dallas, who passed the required test and met the criteria for acceptance into the Special Forces.

However, not all was lost for my friends. After they were made aware of my acceptance in the Special Forces, I learned that all of them—who had attended basic training, AIT, and Jump School with me—were assigned to the 82$^{nd}$ Airborne at Fort Bragg. We were all going to Fort Bragg and would have an opportunity to see one another from time to time.

# Chapter 4

## Home of the 7th and 3rd Special Forces Groups, Fort Bragg, NC

---

After arriving at Fort Bragg and settling in, I inquired about the location of the 3rd Special Forces Group and learned that the unit was only a half mile or so from where I was. A friend of mine from basic training accompanied me to the area where my brother was. When we arrived, we saw people dressed partially in uniform and partially in civilian clothes, my brother among them. Their attire reminded me of the TV show MASH. Their unit appeared to lack discipline, and they seemed to do whatever they wanted, or at least dress any way they wanted. As I was approaching the unit, I saw my brother outside the barracks, and I pulled my hat down to hide my face. I noticed him looking in my direction, and he soon recognized me. I did not tell him that I was attempting to join the Special Forces, and he was surprised and pleased to see me.

It was fun to be around my brother again. To my surprise, he had a car, and it was not long before I was going off post with him.

## Trying to Become One of America's Best

I thought Jump School was the ultimate in testing my physical abilities, but I was about to be physically and mentally pushed further than even I thought I could go. Special Forces training was the most grueling and challenging of all. As a Special Forces trainee, I could wear the green beret, but I could not wear a Special Forces flash or patch on my beret. The patch or flash, as it was called, signified that someone was a school-trained, fully fledged, and unit-assigned Special Forces soldier. Even though we enjoyed wearing the berets, we knew we were not Green Beret soldiers and longed for the day we could be looked upon as full Green Beret soldiers.

Once I began training, I realized there was more classroom training than I had expected. These classes were quite extensive, and the subject matters were as tough as any college course I have ever taken. We went to classes daily for several months, and when we were not in class, we were involved in specialized physical training. Even though the classes were very difficult, I was able to hang on and complete each segment.

Early in training, I had an encounter with one of the sergeants in charge of a squad in our barracks that was also in training. Each morning before class, we were required to clean the barracks. One morning, as I was waiting to get the floor buffer, I told the trainees who were having trouble using it that I would buff the floor if they would give it to me. I figured that, if I waited on them to finish their area, it would take longer than if I just did the whole floor myself. I had almost completed the floor and just had a small area and the cadre room left when the electrical cord to the buffer caught fire. There were approximately forty-five minutes left to get to breakfast prior to class. When the sergeant came in, I told him that the buffer was not working and said that if he could get someone to get another buffer and complete the small area, I could then go to breakfast. To my surprise and amazement, the sergeant told me to go get another buffer and finish the floor myself. I explained that I had volunteered to buff the floor and that it was not my area that needed buffing. He repeated his instructions. I looked around the room and saw that the confrontation had drawn a few spectators, including my acting sergeant. I told the first sergeant, "That's my sergeant, and if he tells me to get a buffer, I will." I caught this acting sergeant off guard, and he did not know what to say. As he stood there hesitating to say any thing, I walked off and went to breakfast.

As I was walking back to the barracks from breakfast, I noticed my actual sergeant walking toward me. As soon as he got close enough, he asked me, "Hargis, what the hell did you do?" As I tried to explain what had happened, he interrupted me, telling me I was never to disobey an order. He also informed me that Sergeant Gray, the sergeant in the barracks whom I had ignored, had gone to the company commander and logged a complaint. My sergeant said that both he and I were in trouble.

We went to the company commander's office. The company commander, who just happened to be a full-bird colonel, did not allow me to say anything to explain myself. However, it appeared he was aware of the facts, and he commenced to chewing me out in a way I had never experienced before. It was brutal. He had the authority to kick me out of the Special Forces training program and threatened to do so. He told me that if I ever did anything like that again, he would ship me off to the 82nd Airborne, which was also domiciled at Bragg, and that would have been embarrassing. I left there with a renewed respect for authority—well, sort of.

We moved into newly constructed barracks that were much different from the old, traditional, wooden barracks, with an old-fashioned coal-burning furnace, no central air, and open bay sleeping. The new ones were all brick, air-conditioned buildings with two-man rooms, which gave us a little more privacy. I was bunked with a White soldier who got the maximum benefit out of wearing the Special Forces uniform. He would tell me about going to small towns off post where the townspeople treated him like a celebrity or royalty. He milked it for all it was worth. Even though this was the first time we had lived together in one room, we got to know each other well. On one occasion, after living together for a while, he confessed something to me. Like most White people in 1965, he did not know any Black people, and the only information he had received was normally negative. He told me that I was quite different from what he had expected. I was a little taken aback and asked him what he meant. He explained that even though he was from Washington state, he had had very little contact with Black people. He added that he saw only negative things on the television and that was the extent of his knowledge of Black people. I explained to him that I was not much different from him and that both of us most likely wanted some of the same things out of life. He seemed to respect what I was saying and began to realize that what he was seeing on television and reading in the newspapers about Black people did not apply to all Black people.

I continued my training, which included a class in Morse code. That class was fun. Not only did we have to learn how to make words from dots and dashes, but we also competed with one another to see how many words we could transmit per minute. I turned out to be good at sending and receiving messages.

Another part of the classroom training that stood out was map reading. It was a vital part of the training and, at times, one of the most difficult classes. We had classes in light weapons, explosives, language, and survival. The survival portion of the training introduced me to edible items, such as tree bark and certain bugs, that I was not aware were edible.

We took many field trips that were designed to test our ability to survive as well as to work in small groups to accomplish missions. On one survival outing, we had a two-man team and were required to travel through simulated enemy territory to reach our targeted destination. We had only one compass, and my partner just happened to be the one who held it. Early in our survival mission, enemy forces captured my partner, so I was without a compass and in an area that included a swamp. I had a general understanding of where I needed to go judging by where the moon was located. By the way, this was a night mission. I approached the swampy area and contemplated trying to swim across it. As I walked along the bank of this small body of water, I hit a swampy area and went under. Vines and all kinds of debris kept me from getting to drier ground, but I finally fought my way out of that mess. That experience convinced me that I needed to find another way to reach my destination. I wandered around for a while, seeking an avenue. While staying out of sight of enemy patrols, I observed the enemy capture some soldiers on my team. As I laid in the brush, staying out of sight, I realized I had to cross the bridge they were patrolling to reach my other team members. As the night stretched on, I learned that the exercise was to end somewhere around midnight, and I knew that time was close. I also figured I could not remain in hiding and had to decide to either attempt to cross the bridge, which would certainly result in my being seen and captured, or cross the bridge with the intent of being captured. Either way I would end my part of the exercise and would not have to worry about trying to find a way to safety, which I did not have a clue on how to reach. As the patrol vehicle crossed the bridge, I snuck in behind it, hoping they would not see me. However, they did, and the enemy soldiers jumped out of the vehicle, grabbed me, threw me to the ground, pushed my face into the dirt, and just generally roughed me up. They took me back to their command unit and began to interrogate me, but within minutes, the exercise was concluded, bringing relief for me. My survival techniques had been tested, and since it was only a stateside exercise, I had passed with flying colors.

On another trip to the field with a group of trainees, we were divided into teams of four, one of whom was designated as team leader. We set out to test our radio operation skills. I did not have a problem getting along with the other soldiers even though I was one of very few Blacks in Special Forces training. I never encountered overt racism. Even though I did not feel discriminated against, I did encounter a problem with the team leader of our group on this exercise. Part of our outing required physical endurance, as well as displaying our radio operator skills. Along with our regular gear, which included a backpack, each member had the responsibility of carrying a ninety-pound generator on his back for a day at a time. On the day I was to carry, which was the second day, I had no problems even though, including my own gear, I was carrying about one hundred pounds. The team member who had carried it the first day also had not had a problem. However, on the third day, the largest and most muscular member of our group complained of being tired after carrying the equipment for several hours. The team leader, for whatever reason, decided to relieve this team member of the load and instructed me to finish the day for him. Now, you must remember the problem I had with the floor buffer situation, and now I had to decide how I was going to handle this latest challenge to my manhood and my principles. I told the team leader, without thinking much about the consequences, that I would not carry the generator. I added that I had carried it on my assigned day and had not asked for any help. I also said that the soldier complaining was much bigger than I am and that he should be able to carry the generator on his designated day. The team leader replied that he was going to report my failure to follow his instructions once we returned to Fort Bragg, and I said that I did not care.

I knew in the back of my mind that I had a good argument but also knew I should have followed instructions. I was caught between the proverbial rock and the hard place and had quite a dilemma on my hands. A few days later, my turn to carry the generator came again. As I had previously, I carried the generator for the entire day. At one point, I stumbled to the ground with the generator on my back while holding onto the tripod stand. My team leader figured I was tired, which I was, and as I regained my balance and kept walking, he said, "You are going to kill yourself trying to prove a point." I told the team leader that it was my day to carry the generator and that was what I was going to do. I was determined that I was going to complete my day with the generator as I expected the others to do. There were no other problems, we had a successful field trip, and I guess I proved my point. After completing our training mission and returning to Fort Bragg, the team leader did not mention anything about the generator incident.

The training also consisted of several paratrooper jumps and jumps from different types of airplanes. I had the opportunity to jump out of a jet airplane, which was one of the first jet jumps. We jumped from a plane called Caribou. The Caribou had a rear tailgate that we jumped from, which was quite a different experience than jumping from the side door of an airplane. Another time, I was first in the "stick," meaning I was the first in line to jump, but jumping first from the tailgate was truly an experience. I also jumped from a helicopter, another unique experience. In that case, many things were different from a plane jump. To prepare for that jump, I sat on the floor of the helicopter, with my feet dangling out, and once I jumped, I fell straight down. When jumping from a regular airplane, the wind force from the jet or propeller would pull you horizontally, and the wind force would cause things to happen faster, including the parachute opening in about ten seconds from the time of the jump. Training allowed us to develop an internal clock to count the seconds until the parachute was to open. As I said, jumping from the helicopter was very different. Once I jumped, my body fell straight down due to there being no prop wind forcing me horizontally. As I was falling straight down, I mentally counted the seconds, but something seemed wrong. I counted past the normal ten seconds for the static line to pull open the parachute, but nothing happened. Based on prior training, after the main chute did not or would not open within the allotted time, I placed my hand on the reserve parachute's brass ring and came very close to activating it. The reserve parachute is worn in the front at waist level, while the main chute is worn on the back. My heart was beating fast as I began to worry about what I was about to do for two main reasons. I had heard stories about the reserve parachute failing to open above a soldier's head, as it should, and instead falling between his legs, entangling with his legs and failing to open. I do not have to explain what happens next if the parachute does not open. The second concern was about the reserve parachute's possibly becoming entangled with the main chute if it was delayed but finally opened. As the story goes, once you decide the main chute has malfunctioned, you then open the reserve chute. The reserve chute opens correctly, and then the delayed main chute unexpectedly opens, causing the two parachutes to become entangled and both parachutes to collapse. My fear soon subsided. Just before pulling the rip cord for the reserve, the main parachute opened, and I floated safely to the ground. Now that was an experience! It was the most harrowing until I made my first night jump.

Most paratrooper jumps were made from C-130 cargo airplanes. One outing that I remember vividly was a contour flight. As we entered the airplane, we took our seats for what we thought was an outing to make a normal jump. However, we soon found out this was a very different flight, and it almost made me sick. Let me explain. Part of my stay at Fort Bragg involved nightclub nightlife. On the night before the contour flight, I had been out at the local E-4 Club, drinking and partying. I knew we had a flight the next morning but did not think there would be any problems making it since this was not the first time I had gone partying prior to making a jump or going up in an airplane. However, what I was about to experience was unlike anything I had previously experienced. I was strapped in for this flight, mentally preparing for the time the green light would come on, the jumpmaster would yell, "Get ready!" and then I would stand, place my parachute cable to a static line, and prepare to jump. But what happened was nothing—at least, no jump took place. We sat there as the pilot simulated flying under combat conditions and flew the plane at about treetop level. When flying that low to the ground, the pilot had to make several quick maneuvers to avoid hitting trees and rolling with the hills. The flight followed the contour of the earth, and the pilot rolled, dipped, and elevated to maintain the same distance from the ground as he flew. As you may have surmised, we were thrown around inside the plane as the pilot made his maneuvers. I probably would have faired all right under normal circumstances, but my condition was not what you would call normal. The whiskey I had drunk the night before was rising in my throat, and I really thought I was going to embarrass myself by vomiting. The embarrassment would have come from all those macho paratroopers' laughing at me for not being able to handle the contour flight. Even though I could taste the whiskey again as it was rising in my throat, it did not rise any higher and I survived the flight. I was glad to get back on the ground. You would think I would modify my behavior, especially just before going up in an airplane, but I was young and foolish. I felt that if I had to do it again, I would deal with the circumstances better. I could not stay out of the clubs.

Speaking of the E-4 Club, Fort Bragg was very good about bringing in talented musicians for us to listen and dance to. There was one blind performer who frequented the E-4 Club name Ronnie Millsap. In later years, he became a famous country and western singer, but at Fort Bragg, he sang a different tune. Thursday nights featured soul music, and Black soldiers dominated the club. The club played a different kind of music on Friday and Saturday nights that attracted people of another persuasion.

Ronnie Millsap was very accomplished at singing songs previously recorded and performed by Stevie Wonder, Otis Redding, Wilson Pickett, Ray Charles, and many more. He was phenomenally talented. We also had occasion to see better-known performers at the E-4 Club like Major Lance and the Drifters. The night the Drifters performed, something happened that was reminiscent of something I had seen in an old cowboy movie.

As my brother and I were sitting in the back of the club enjoying the music, someone in the balcony area dropped a glass down on someone near the dance floor. Then somebody downstairs threw something to the balcony area, and the next thing we knew a chair was coming from the balcony downstairs and all hell broke loose. Soldiers inside the club were throwing bottles and glasses all over the place. Several fights broke out, and it appeared everybody was fighting. My brother and I maneuvered farther to the rear of the club to get out of harm's way. However, the way things were going, there was no safe haven inside the club. As we were standing at the back, somebody threw a bottle in our direction and hit a guy standing near us. The message was clear—we needed to exit the club if we wanted to remain uninjured. It was fortunate that we left the club when we did because, shortly after we exited, the military police showed up and began arresting everybody inside. We stood outside and saw many of our acquaintances loaded into paddy wagons. What a night.

Speaking of fighting, there was one soldier whom we labeled the singing cook because he was a mess hall cook and liked to sing when he was serving in the chow line. One other thing about him was that he loved to fight. This soldier was about six foot two or three and probably weighed about 190 pounds. He was not that big based on today's standards, but he was fearless and loved to fight. And he was right in the middle of the melee at the E-4 Club when we were supposed to be enjoying the Drifters. He also loved to dance—or do something like dancing. Long before anyone was doing the freeze on the dance floor, the singing cook was doing it. We would all be on the dance floor doing our thing, and suddenly, the singing cook would freeze and remain in that position for the longest time. We thought he was crazy, but no one was willing to call him crazy because they would have to fight him if they did. He was a fun person to be around unless there was a fight he could get into.

Back to Special Forces training. On a very clear night, we were scheduled to make a night jump. It was my first night jump, and I was somewhat apprehensive (scared) about doing it. It was scary enough when I could see where I was going and where I was landing. As we boarded the airplane, we went through our normal checklist prior to making the jump. However, something went wrong, which I could have predicted, knowing it was not going to be an easy night out. The pilot came over the intercom and explained that, due to a bad approach over the drop zone, we could not make the jump as planned. He informed us that he had to fly over the DZ again for us to make our jump. Normally the pilot would make two passes over the DZ, with half of us jumping out on the first pass and the next half jumping out on the second. Due to pilot error, we all had to jump out of the plane on one pass, which was not an easy task. Those who were near the end of what we called the stick could very possibly land in trees rather than in the DZ, which was normally a wide-open, sandy space. Since we had only one pass, it was important that we speed up our exit even though there were inherent dangers in doing so. What I was about to experience reinforced those fears.

When my turn came to jump, I went as closely behind the soldier in front of me as possible. That was not the problem; the problem was the person behind me. I looked up as I was exiting the airplane and noticed that my parachute had partially opened. Before it was fully engaged, the trooper behind me landed on it. My first thought was that he was going to collapse my partially open parachute; therefore, my life was in danger. As I continued looking up, my parachute popped open, and the trooper who had landed on it slid off and shot by me like a bullet—because his parachute had not opened. His was in what we called a streamer, a parachute that does not open even though it is outside its cover bag. I was relieved that my parachute had opened, but I was in fear for the other paratrooper. It appeared that his life was now in jeopardy. We both had angels jumping with us that night, though. As I looked down at him, his parachute finally opened right before my eyes, and I was thoroughly relieved for the second time in short order. However, the events of the night were not over, not yet. As I prepared for my landing, I was not able to see much on the ground, even on this bright moonlit night. Because I could not maneuver my parachute to land in a better place, I landed in a thornbush. However, that did not bother me much; I was just happy to be alive, on the ground, and in one piece. What a night.

I struggled with my classwork mainly because I had not developed the necessary study skills required to be a good student and I did not give up the nightlife. While in class, I understood the instructions given, but I maintained a bad habit that I had developed in high school—I did not practice or study the information provided me. As a result, I was not sure I would pass my final exams and graduate. I studied harder toward the end and for the final examination. After completing the examination, I sat in the classroom with the other trainees, listening to names being called out in grade order. I did not have a clue whether I had scored high enough on my final examination to graduate from Special Forces School/Special Warfare School or whether I would become a full-fledged Special Forces soldier. Toward the end of the list, they called my name, and it was one of the most gratifying moments of my young life. I could now wear the green beret with distinction, knowing I had completed all required elements of training. As a young man who had grown up in the government projects on the east side of Fort Worth; who had graduated from Dunbar High School located in Stop Six, Texas; who was now a graduate from the Special Warfare School in Fort Bragg with silver wings on my chest and the coveted green beret on my head, I felt like I had conquered the world and accomplished something that I could not even dream of doing.

# Chapter 5

## Reality Check

———◆◆◆———

I was so happy about graduating from the Special Forces School that I failed to focus on the fact that the year was 1966 and I was behind the cotton curtain in North Carolina.

Those of us who had just graduated got the rest of the day off and set out to celebrate downtown. The town of Fayetteville, North Carolina, was segregated. The group went to have our celebratory meal at a place that most of the White soldiers had frequented but that was not familiar to me. I was driving my brother's car, and as I pulled into the restaurant parking lot and started walking across it, I noticed a man approach one of the soldiers. They appeared to be looking at me, and I felt that something was going down. However, neither of them said anything to me, so I continued into the establishment. Once inside, a waitress came over to our table, where I was sitting with three White soldiers, and took our orders. As time passed, we noticed that the other tables were receiving service while we weren't, and those at my table soon realized that all was not well. One of the graduates got up to inquire about our meal, and we soon understood what it meant to still be living in the segregated South. The manager told the graduate that he could not serve our table while I was there. I was the lone Black Special Forces soldier in the entire group. The graduate came over and told the group what was said. They appeared to be somewhat upset, but only one of them left with me. He just happened to be the one White person I had met in basic training who was also accepted for Special Forces training. Plus, he had ridden to the restaurant with me. The two of us went to the "colored" section of town and had a hamburger and a beer. So much for the idea of a fancy graduation party. I was still just one Black soldier among a multitude of White soldiers. I had developed relationships with many of my peers but never achieved the closeness one would feel from those of similar persuasions.

Fort Bragg was home to the 3rd and 7th Special Forces Groups. The 8th Group was stationed in Panama; the 9th was stationed in Europe. We all knew the 5th Special Forces Group was in Vietnam, but we were excited about where we might be assigned. As I expected, I was to remain at Fort Bragg; I received orders to report to Company B, 7th Special Forces Group.

Fort Bragg was also home to several famous named DZs. Some were named for sites of paratrooper landings during WWII, like Sicily, Omaha, and Normandy.

The introduction to my assigned Special Forces unit began with a company formation early one morning when we met the unit command. Our top sergeant, who happened to be a sergeant major, quickly made us aware of who was in charge of our unit. He went before the group and emphatically told us that he was in charge and that he kept some officers around, those standing behind him, to sign papers. Now that was impressive, and it was true. However, we knew what rank was. In fact, there was plenty of rank in our unit. The company commander was a major, and the top sergeant who was a sergeant major was not the only one in our unit. Shortly after graduation, we all received promotions to sergeant. I was officially a Special Forces sergeant. To put that in perspective, my brother, not being school trained as I was, could rise only to the specialist rank. I was proud to be a buck sergeant. As a newly graduated Special Forces soldier, I was assigned to a twelve member A-team to work with a more seasoned radio operator. Most of us had other duties assigned as well. Our unit was seeking someone to volunteer to perform mail-delivery service, so I volunteered, as did one other. We were required to take a test to get certified to handle US mail. I passed the test and assumed the duties. As the newly appointed mail soldier, I was responsible for setting up a delivery system. I had my own little room, where I worked the mail and delivered it to soldiers. The room was set apart from other areas where activities were going on, and friends dropped by to visit on occasion. Some of my White friends hung out with me to escape other things or just to hang out. One day, some of my basic training friends came up from the 82nd Airborne to visit me. They were a lively and loud group. When they came in, I changed my behavior to conform to theirs, and my White friend, who was now surrounded by a group of loud, shit-talking brothers, had to ease out. If I had kept behaving the way I had while with my White friend, just imagine how and what the visitors from the 82nd Airborne would have labeled me. Being one of very few Blacks in the Special Forces, I ascribed to the concept, "When in Rome, do as the Romans."

During the summer at Bragg, I learned about weekend warriors when we were invaded by a group of National Guard/ Special Forces who came down from New York to train with us.

I was not familiar with the National Guard, but I soon came to realize that this was a highly educated group that included, doctors, lawyers, and accountants, and they seemed to be mostly, if not all, Jewish. I did not know how the system worked at that time, but I later learned that the privileged few with the right connections joined the National Guard to avoid going into or being drafted into military service—thus, no Vietnam.

I met another Black soldier named Rudy Stewart who had graduated in a different class, and he was from New York. Based on our mutual need to embrace our blackness, we developed a close relationship. However, I also developed friendly relationships with several of the White soldiers. One was with a soldier named Krantz. We were very cordial toward each other and talked often. At one point, he went home on leave, and upon his return, he was clearly avoiding me. It was obvious he did not want to talk to me, so I confronted him one day and inquired as to what the problem was. He reluctantly told me that, while he was home on leave, he learned that a Black man had raped his grandmother. I took exception to what he was saying, asking him what that incident had to do with me. We both knew the answer, but he could not give me a definitive answer. Even though I believe he realized he could not associate the rape with me, our relationship was not the same from that point forward. I also realized that what I experienced with Krantz was not unique; some people in White America stereotyped Black Americans. How unfortunate—I really thought a lot of Krantz.

I met this other White soldier by the name of Richard Reinhardt, who was from New Jersey. He was not all that friendly, but he was at least decent. We played on the same flag football team, and he was one heck of a wide receiver. He was slow of foot, so I could never understand how he was always open on pass routes. The quarterback seemed to find him open often and was able to get the ball to him. At that time, I was quite ignorant regarding precise route running, while he had been schooled in the art. He was a popular guy and had a car on post. He gave me a ride one day as I was walking to the area where we were to play a flag football game. I guess he felt obligated; he asked me if I wanted a ride, I accepted, and we were on our way. One of the soldiers in the vehicle, who must have known him back in New Jersey, asked him if he still had his dog named Nigger. It got very quiet in the car, and Richard was decent enough to change the subject, but I could not believe what I had heard. Could you imagine someone naming a dog Nigger? He obviously lived in a segregated neighborhood in New Jersey. Also, can you imagine the other person having nerve enough to ask the question in my presence? I felt like Rodney Dangerfield in his prime—no respect. I did not say anything and learned a valuable lesson about self-constraint.

Special Forces training included of going on field trips to hone our skills. During one such trip, a group of us were crossing a small stream with water so clear and pretty that we just had to get a drink from it. Our supply unit had given us pills to purify water retrieved from streams and other bodies of water, but this water was so clear and clean looking that we just knew nothing was wrong with it. Later that night, my body told me something different. I had to make an emergency deposit. I went up on a nearby hill, far enough away from our campsite that I would not wake up or disturb the others, and I commenced to losing about fifteen pounds. I was truly sick, obviously from drinking bacteria-filled water. I learned another valuable lesson.

On another field trip, we loaded into the backs of deuce-and-a-quarter trucks and headed to someplace unknown. We soon found out it was a test of endurance. About halfway to our destination, we were told to dismount the trucks and walk the remainder of the trip. At the time, we did not know that we were only halfway there, and it was approximately two o'clock when we hit the ground. We walked all night long, and I thought I was just going to die; I was so tired and sleepy. I did not know it at the time, but the trip was planned to see how we would handle staying up more than twenty-four hours and walking approximately twenty-five miles. All I remember is falling asleep when we came to a stop, and while I was sleeping, something bit me on my upper lip that caused it to swell up to twice its size. I cannot recall what took place afterward, but I do know that the little nap, spider bite and all, refreshed me enough to finish out the day.

Another first that I experienced while living in the barracks at Fort Bragg was the bitter winter cold. We did not have electric or gas-powered furnaces to keep us warm, and in fact this was my first experience with "black face." Soldiers, both Black and White, were required to load the coal-fired furnace. I mostly saw the White soldiers who were on furnace duty; after they shoveled coal into the furnaces, they were covered with coal soot—thus the black face. It was quite a sight, and no one complained.

North Carolina had very cold winters, much colder than what I was accustomed to. On a particularly cold night, the barracks heater was nonfunctional, so we did not have any heat. I put on my full field gear, which consisted of my fatigues, a field jacket, wool socks, gloves, and a warm cap, as well as anything else I could find, prior to going to bed. I was somewhat warm. At the time, I did not have a sleeping bag, but those who did slept comfortably without having to put on all of their gear. However, it got so cold in the barracks that night that the water in the butt cans froze solid. Now that was cold.

The infamous Sergeant Gray, whom I spoke of earlier, and I became friends. He was the same sergeant who had reported me for failing to follow his instructions in the buffer situation. Not only did we become friends, but we soon got in trouble together. Sergeant Gray asked me to ride off post with him one day. I knew I did not have permission, but he was a seasoned soldier and I thought he knew what he was doing. We were gone most of the morning, and during that time, the company sergeant major was looking for me. As soon as I returned, I was called to the office and questioned regarding my whereabouts. I told the sergeant major that I had taken a ride downtown with Sergeant Gray, as if to say that since I was with him it must have been all right. Sergeant Gray became responsible for my being chewed out for the first and second time in my army career. the sergeant major told me I was not to leave post without prior permission. That chewing out also consisted of a few adjectives to command my attention.

Sergeant Gray was a heavy drinker, and during one wild drinking party, I learned about blackouts. We had a company party, which obviously included only men. We had all types of liquor and beer to drink. I drank my share of the spirits, but I believe Sergeant Gray drank part of someone else's. The strange thing was that, even though Sergeant Gray seemed to be a little high, he did not appear to be drunk. He drove me to my destination off post and did not seem to have any problems driving. However, and to my surprise, the next day he asked me how I had gotten home. Initially, I thought he was joking, but when I realized he was not, I told him he had taken me. I did not know what had happened and thought he had just lost it, but later I learned that he had a blackout. Sergeant Gray and I became such good friends that, when the NCO Club presented him with two tickets for dinner to honor his birthday, he invited me to accompany him to the NCO Club. I had come a long way from being sent to the principal's office in my relationship with Sergeant Gray.

I was scheduled to make my last jump prior to ending my career as a Special Forces paratrooper. I always had this fear of being killed on my last jump. I am not sure, but I would bet that most troopers had the same feeling. The last jump was uneventful, with the exception of my hitting the ground all wrong, falling flat on my face, getting a mouth full of sand, and losing my helmet and my watch as I hit the ground. I was so happy that I was in one piece, I ran off the DZ and did not concern myself with the watch that had come off. Free at last, free at last, thank God almighty, free at last.

As I was closing in on the end of my army career, the army made a sales pitch to keep me in. They offered me ten thousand dollars to re-up. The recruiter explained that the ten thousand was a bonus, and my next year's salary would earn interest while I was serving in Vietnam. His persuasion included a trip to Vietnam for a year and the fact that I would not need any income during that period. The recruitment proposal also included a promotion to sergeant E-6 and the possibility of another promotion to E-7 upon my return to the States. The offer was very tempting, and I gave it considerable thought. I finally decided I would not take it; after taking everything into consideration, I decided it was in my best interest to go home. What I had been reading in the army newspaper, The Stars and Stripes, played into my decision. During March and April of 1967, numerous Special Forces camps fell to Viet Cong insurgents, and many newly in-country Special Forces soldiers were being killed. So I had to think long and hard. The Star and Stripes would list the names of soldiers who were recently killed in Vietnam, which was sobering, especially because some of those names were people I knew. It did not take me long to realize that it was in the interest of my health to turn down the army's recruiting offer and catch the first thing smoking to head for home.

When processing out of the army, all of us who were leaving the service had to go to the separation station, just as we had gone to the induction station when we first entered. I saw almost the same group of guys processing out that I had seen processing in. The sergeant in charge of the separation station placed me in charge of those soldiers processing out the army since I was one of very few sergeants and the only Special Forces sergeant processing out that day. I was reunited with some of the same group I had been with in basic training, AIT, and Jump School, including some of those who had come to my unit to visit me. The army had had an adverse effect on one in the group, the one from Watts. He did not seem to mellow while in the service; rather, service had seemed to harden him. At the separation station, he and another soldier from our earlier days got into an altercation. As I was in charge, I had to keep order. The soldier from Watts pulled a large knife and began to chase the other soldier. He caught up with him and held the knife to his throat. In observing this, I was not sure if he was going to cut the other soldier's throat or not. It did not appear that he was playing, though, so I had to intercede. I approached the soldier from Watts and convinced him to put the knife away. He did not appear to be the same person I had grown to know through our training sessions, but I had to see if I could still command his respect. To my pleasant surprise, he put away the knife as if to say that he still respected me and my position of authority. I believe our whole group, which consisted of about ten of us, was as surprised that he responded to me as I was. It soon became clear that he had developed quite a reputation during his stay in the 82nd Airborne. I was not dealing with the same person from Watts I thought I knew. When he came into the army, he was a tough guy, but while he was in the army, he had developed a mean streak and what appeared to be a killer mentality. I often wonder what happened to him. Anyway, I was soon on my way back to Fort Worth, and I left the army feeling like a lean, mean killing machine, light on the killing. I was taking all my military training back to the civilian world, and I wondered how I would use that training in future endeavors.

# Chapter 6

## Headed Home

During my tenure in the military, my family had moved back to Texas once my dad was unable to work any longer due to illness and retired on disability. In addition, while I was in the early stages of my Special Forces training, my mother, who had been fighting a long battle with leukemia, died. My life had taken another unexpected turn, and I had to grow up and take my life more seriously. I was returning home under very different circumstances than I had left.

I was returning to Texas during the turbulent sixties, the Vietnam War was still going strong, and race relations were at the forefront of issues facing the United States of America. As I went to the airport and boarded the airplane, I quickly realized that many eyes were on me for one reason and one reason only. It was the uniform. Not many people had seen a Special Forces Green Beret, especially a Black one. During my flight home, a very telling event took place. Many military personnel were aboard the aircraft, and after a few drinks, people got friendly. I became friendly with a few White soldiers, and they became very friendly with the female flight attendants. I was also joking around with the attendants, who just happened to be White.

During the flight, the soldiers set up a rendezvous in Dallas with the female attendants and invited me to join them. I was not sure what part of the country the soldiers or the attendants were from, but I knew that what they were expecting of me would not happen when we landed in Dallas. The year was 1967, and we were still in the racially segregated South. I made some lame excuse and did not accompany the group to their fun location. However, as I arrived in Dallas, eyes were still on the Green Beret.

After arriving at Love Field in Dallas, I walked through the airport, I realized I was still being closely observed because of my Special Forces uniform. However, I also knew I would soon have that chapter of my life behind me, and I could no longer capitalize on the uniform.

I returned to Fort Worth and needed to decide on my future. I had a few dollars in my pocket and decided to take it easy for a few weeks before seeking employment. I had the GI Bill at my disposal but did not consider going to college at that time. After about a month of partying and drinking every day, my money started running low and I decided to seek employment.

Since the Vietnam conflict was still going strong, there were still great employment opportunities in the defense industry. A local defense contractor, General Dynamics (GD), was in a continuous hiring mode and just happened to have a hiring ad in the local newspaper for aircraft assemblers. Prior experience was not necessary, and the company would train.

I went down to the local employment office to apply. Once there, the employment people administered aptitude and dexterity tests. After I passed the tests, one of the employment officers interviewed me. The officer asked me what job I was interested in, and I advised him that I was applying for the aircraft assembler position advertised in the newspaper. I soon realized that military service did not change the racist attitudes of those who felt some authority over Blacks. The employment officer asked me if I would accept a janitor's job if an assembler job were not available. I had just finished the dexterity and aptitude tests, but then I had to pass a test that was obviously set aside for Black applicants. My mother did not raise no dummy, so I answered that I would accept a janitor's position if an assembler position were not available. I also realized that, if I had answered no to that question, I probably would have remained out of work.

I reported to GD to complete the application process and, yes, I was being processed in for an assembler position. Once there, I still had more tests to pass. I took a physical, which included an eye examination and a urine specimen. I wore glasses, and without them, I was nearly blind, so that information was noted on the eye examination. When the time came for me to pee in a cup, I was unable to provide the specimen. The young Human Resources employee, a White male, who was processing me in took the opportunity to needle me about my eyesight and my inability to provide the required urine specimen. He called me "no see, no pee Hargis." His comments were unprofessional and another unwarranted, racist test to see how I would deal with adversity. I only glanced at him when he made the comment. I did not respond, knowing that if I said anything, I would be labeled another Black man with an attitude.

I was hired, and the company put me in a month-long training program. I was one of two Black men in the class and the only one to complete the training. The other person did not take the class as seriously as I did and was not among the group graduating.

During the training, I met a White person in the class who befriended me. During one conversation, he told me something that has remained with me since that time. He told me that I was blessed with an inherent talent. He was one of those White people with the opinion that all Black people had special talent. He was more than likely speaking of some physical abilities, but at the time, I thought he really saw something in me even though I had not demonstrated anything, to the best of my knowledge, to lead him to believe that. I have always made positives out negatives, even though sometimes I was rather naive about what was really going on. In retrospect, I believe that was one of those times. Either way, this was the first integrated school setting in Fort Worth in which I had participated, and what he said resonated with me at the time. After the class was over, the instructor asked me if I knew why the other Black person in the class had not passed. It seemed he was trying to make sure, as much as he could, that he had given the other guy a fair opportunity and at the same time seeking my approval or understanding. I assured him that, based on my observation, he had been fair.

After attending class for approximately a month, I went to the plant to begin my career as a tube bender. I had also taken the postal examination during the first few weeks after returning home and gave little thought of going to work for the post office. After being in the aircraft industry for another three weeks, I was surprised to get a call from the post office offering me a job. I now had a decision to make. Should I stay on the job I had been on for almost two months, or should I go to the post office and start all over on a new job? I considered several factors in making my decision.

I was single and did not have enough seniority to remain on the day shift at GD, but night work was not for me at that stage of my life. I was also concerned with layoffs and knew the Vietnam conflict would not last forever; therefore, layoffs were inevitable. I made the decision to quit my job at GD and report for duty with the post office.

# Chapter 7

## First Stage of Going Postal

My Special Forces military training would serve me well in my career at the post office. I learned what the phrase "going postal" really meant to me and for me. I was about to go postal in the first few days of my employment.

On July 29, 1967, I reported for duty at the main US Post Office in downtown Fort Worth. The post office hired me as a part-time flexible (PTF) city carrier, and the main post office where I worked at the time had a letter carrier unit upstairs in the main building. However, prior to reporting to my new job as a city letter carrier, I had to deal with the employment office manager, who was a woman and did not seem to be very nice, especially to minorities. When I was still working at GD had to take a physical prior to reporting to the post office, I did not want to miss a day of work and asked my father to take the medical report to the post office. He did as I asked, and when I got home from work, he told me, "That lady down there told me to tell you if you wanted that job, then you needed to bring your own information to the personnel office." The way he explained it to me, she evidently did not like his bringing the information to her and that my job might not be a sure thing. Well, I reported when directed and was hired.

I trained for a few weeks, during which time I encountered some people who were friendly and some who were not so friendly. Again, you must understand, the year was 1967 and I was one of only two Blacks of about thirty carriers scheduled to report for duty on that date. The workforce had been integrated for some time, but some individuals were still fighting the Civil War. I could feel their disapproval about working alongside Blacks.

I delivered mail out of a car supplied by the General Services Administration (GSA), and I did not have a uniform to identify myself as mail carrier. I drove around visualizing myself as a GSA employee with an important job, but I was a letter carrier.

After dealing with subtle racism during the training period and surviving it, I reported for duty at Berry Street Station, which was on the west side of town, and at that time the area was predominately White. The significance of being assigned to this area will become clearer later. At the time there was just one Black carrier at Berry Street Station when Van Malone and I were assigned.

In my early days as a mail carrier, the work consisted of assisting regular carriers in the office with casing mail and carrying their handoff mail, what we called swings, to the street. PTF carriers were assigned swings when the regular carriers had too much mail to deliver within a specified period. On occasion, PTF carriers delivered full routes when regular carriers would took time off for vacation or other leave. As PTFs, we were assigned in a way that provided us an opportunity to work on various routes and to meet most of the carriers in the office.

On a few routes, the carrier had to take the city bus to the beginning of the route. One day, I rode the bus, and the bus driver was very talkative and had quite a sense of humor. He said that he had picked up a few habits as a bus driver that affected him in his personal life, including that, on occasion, he would be driving his personal vehicle and see someone sitting at a bus stop, and he found himself pulling over to pick them up. We had a good laugh about that. Something similar happened to me, actually. The duties of a PTF carrier included making collection runs in the late afternoons after we finished mail delivery for the day. These runs would take me all over my delivery zone collecting mail to transport to the main post office for processing. After making collection runs over a period of months, I developed the bus driver's syndrome. I found myself almost pulling over in my personal vehicle when I saw a mailbox on a corner. I do not know if I ever actually pulled over, but I know I was close a few times.

On one of the early days at Berry Street Station, while assisting on a route, I overheard a conversation between two White carriers. One said to the other, "What do you call that thing we used as kids to throw or sling rocks?" The other replied, "That's called a nigger shooter." I was still in my probationary period, and for fear of being fired, I knew I could not respond to the derogatory comment. I just made a mental note of who made the comment.

On another occasion, I overheard another carrier explaining how times were changing. He told a coworker that his dad had told him about a Black person who was hired as a firefighter and mentioned the fact that firefighters have to live in the same facility. He added that his father commented that, evidently, a better group of Blacks was entering the service workforce. I was only a few feet away from them. I was certain that the conversation was designed and intended for me, but I was not sure what message they were trying to send me. I again took note.

Many interesting things took place at Berry Street. People openly made racist remarks about Black women. One older White carrier, who was obviously mean-spirited, stated that Black women were too lazy to get up and use a douche after having sex so they just lay there and got pregnant. I could not believe what I was hearing, but this was 1967. If ever I wanted to challenge an individual and use some of the techniques I had learned while training as a Special Forces soldier, this was the time. But I may have been wise beyond my twenty-three years because I knew I could not even challenge this person verbally. I was still serving a probationary period, and I knew I would be the one faulted if I spoke up or acted out.

I faced other challenges when I went to the street to carry mail. Customers would say things to me to which I could not respond for fear of losing my job. In the early days of delivering mail, I had customers who claimed to know the Fort Worth postmaster and threaten me with the loss of my job for delivering the mail later to them than what they were accustomed to, even though there may have been a legitimate reason for the delay. As a relatively new carrier and not knowing the ropes, I did not know if they could get me fired or not. In most cases, I believed what they were saying. I expected to walk into the office on any given day after delivering my mail and be told that I was fired based on a report from people I believed were racist customers. In fact, one customer moved her mailbox to the back door after she learned that Black carriers were delivering mail in the neighborhood. Another lady approached me one day and asked me where a certain street was, and at that time I knew only the streets where I had actually carried mail. So I told the lady that I did not know where the street was, and she replied in a polite tone, "You're a dumb mailman." I am not sure her comment was racially motivated, but at that time, I felt dumb and thought maybe it was my job to know all the streets in that area. I was repeatedly call mail boy instead of mailman, but that was just a sign of the times.

One day when I was on a collection run, which were assigned to PTF carriers in the late afternoon, I opened the collection box just as a gust of wind came up and blew several letters into the air. I had no way of knowing where the mail went, and I was just sure somebody saw the incident. I figured they would report me, and I would truly lose my job. Now that was real airmail.

On my first Christmas with the post office, I was assigned to deliver packages. Berry Street delivered mail in a very affluent part of town, and it seemed most everyone received numerous packages. The Postal Service did not have enough trucks to deliver all the packages, so they procured old military vehicles that did not have license plates or any kind of ID other than obviously being military. As I was driving one of the loaned vehicles, I was pulled over by the police for driving an unlicensed vehicle. I had to contact the station manager to get the officer to allow me to continue delivering packages. I was not sure how that was going to turn out.

After working a year and finishing my probationary period, things only got more interesting. By then I had developed a decent working relationship with several carriers in the office. In addition, Van Malone and I had become good friends and hung out together after work.

Van and I became pretty good letter carriers. We hated working on Saturdays and would have much rather been drinking beer and watching football games. When we were assigned to work on Saturdays, the supervisors knew that they were going to get maximum effort out of us so that we could finish and go home. Supervisors liked our efforts because they were responsible for getting the mail delivered within the fewest hours. Supervisors' performance was measured by the number of office and delivery hours used each week. Saturday was the first day of the delivery week, and if they started out using a minimum number of hours, that would normally put them in good shape for the rest of the week. Van and I gave them that advantage on most Saturdays we worked.

We also enjoyed getting off work by at least by noon on Saturdays, so when we went out on our assigned routes, we would race to see who could get back the earliest. Most days, we wouldn't return to the office until at least two thirty or three o'clock. Saturdays were usually low-volume mail days, which would allow us to complete delivery earlier anyway, but for the two of us, ages twenty-three and twenty-four, we were able to put on the afterburners and really get out there and deliver mail. On many occasions, we jumped off porches, jumped over bushes, left the vehicles running while making deliveries, and basically broke every safety rule written in an effort to get back by that magical twelve o'clock and get home during the first quarter of the televised game. Those were fun days, but looking back, they were also dangerous days because of all the safety violations we had committed.

I was proud of the fact that I was good at carrying mail. I was not the swiftest carrier in the office, but once on the street, I could really get around my routes. On one occasion, I was assigned to the route of one of the senior carriers. I had often heard it was one of the shorter routes in the office, especially since this senior carrier knew how to stretch his efforts out in the office and on the street. The route consisted of about three hours in the office and about five hours on the street. On this day, I was assigned to just carry the route. I reported to work around eight o'clock and was on the street by about eight-thirty. I knew the route was short and that I needed to slow my pace down for two reasons. One was to work enough hours that day to justify coming in. Normally four hours was sufficient. The second reason was that I did not want to show up the regular carrier (too much) on the route. If I carried the route too quickly, it would appear that the regular carrier was not doing much work, and I would then have to deal with him, as they often tried to intimidate PTF carriers.

After leaving the office, I stopped by a drugstore and had breakfast. It was one of several business establishments on this route to which I delivered mail. I stayed there at least thirty minutes before getting back to work. The route was a walking route on which the mail for delivery was stored in green boxes that were placed on street corners. As I completed one segment of the route, I would go to the storage box to get mail for the next section. At approximately eleven o'clock, I had completed the route; however, I was not sure I had carried all the mail. I walked back over the entire route and examined each storage box to make sure I had gotten all the mail out to be delivered. I had delivered it all, so now I had a dilemma. Should I to go back to the office early after working only about three hours and really show up the regular carrier, or should I come up with a way to stay out on the route? I chose the latter. I went back by the drugstore to have lunch. I would not normally eat two meals that close together, but I had an unusual situation on my hands and had to do something to kill time. I was in no hurry as I ate lunch, and once finished I walked back to the station as slowly as I could. In fact, the supervisor of the unit was driving down the street, saw me, and later told me he had to compare me with a utility pole to see if I was moving. I still made it back to the office after a little over four hours, even after taking two thirty-minute-plus breaks and walking the route twice. Despite my best efforts, the senior carrier was still mad at me for what he called "running the route," thereby making him look bad.

In 1967 and 1968, I was still single and staying out late, especially on Friday nights. On one Friday, a good friend of mine got married, and we were up late after the wedding. I needed to decide whether to go home to get a little sleep or just stay up to report to work at 4:00 a.m. It took me a long time to make up my mind, and I eventually left the after party at about two o'clock in the morning and got home in time to get about one hour of good sleep. At the party, I had a few too many drinks and was not quite sober when I woke up, but I was determined to go to work. I drove to work, and my line of travel took me by the house of a female clerk that worked at Berry Street Station. She just happened to be leaving for work at the time I was driving by her house, which was on a conner that intersected with Berry Street.

She saw me as I was driving by and later told me I was all over the road. She said that she decided to follow behind me to ensure I got to work without killing myself. I made it to work all right, despite my obvious impairment. After seeing my condition up close and personal, the female clerk encouraged me to go home before the boss came in. I told her that the boss was a drunk too and that he would not discipline me for coming to work slightly impaired. Nevertheless, she continued in her effort to get me to go home. In the first part of the morning, I was on my feet sorting parcel post and doing what I thought was an okay job. But later that morning I attempted to sit on a stool to case, or process, mail but had a problem staying on the stool with no back support. My balance was not what it should have been while sitting. I did better while standing—slightly better. Soon I realized I was not sobering up enough to perform my duties effectively or efficiently. I began to worry about what the boss would say and decided to take sick leave or, as we called it in those days, drunk leave, and went home. I feared that the boss would be angry at me and would call me to see if I was indeed sick or really at home. I kept the telephone nearby and slept the whole day. I never got the call I was expecting.

As I said, the carrier foreman was a drinker. During the Christmas holidays, it was not uncommon for customers to offer carriers a hot toddy, especially when it was very cold. Many carriers coming off the streets during the holiday season had a few drinks under their belts. My supervisor and one of the carriers at Berry Street co-owned a bus they had converted into a mobile home and bar. During the holidays they would drive the bus on postal property and charge us admission to get on. Once on board, we could drink all the liquor we wanted. I recall getting on the bus one Christmas but do not recall much about getting off. I was not the only one. The next day after returning to work, the supervisor asked his friend which one of them had driven the bus home. Now that is tying one on.

I had not learned my lesson. I continued my partying ways, and on one Saturday morning, it all came crashing down. After partying for about two weeks straight, without getting one night of decent sleep, I went to work very tired. I walked the route but had difficulty keeping my eyes open. I bumped into trees and bushes while attempting to deliver mail. I know that if anyone had seen me walking, they would have known I had one or two too many. I was a complete mess. However, there is an old religious saying that more than likely prevailed. That saying is that God takes care of babies and fools. I was twenty-three or -four—too old to be a baby—and therefore, I must have been the latter. Suddenly, it began to thunder. God's voice woke me, and I was not sleepwalking anymore. Since I did not have sense enough to take care of myself, God intervened. I went home, went straight to bed, and did not wake up until Sunday afternoon. I learned my lesson and modified my behavior accordingly.

After working at Berry Street for several months, I noticed another Black carrier was hired. Like brothers normally do, we kind of sized each other up prior to saying anything. His name was Herron Hudson and over time, we became very good friends. He visited my home and I basically hung out at his place on the weekends. We became very close friends and spent a lot of off time together. Later, he left Berry Street to take a job as a Postal Police Officer, as he was a Military Police while serving in the Air Force. Our friendship continued, however.

Things were rocking along quite well at Berry Street, and I had quite a few White friends. One carrier by the name of Jackie

Gillis took me under his wing and even attempted to teach me to play golf. I also spent many afternoons drinking beer at his home.

Another carrier by the name of Bob Young was a bit older than me but seemed to like me, at least from a distance. He exhibited racial prejudices but liked me for some reason. We often argued just about anything, but when we did argue it was in such a way that we had fun doing it. He had a body like a boxer and enjoyed throwing punches at me, but I had quick hands that gave him a little trouble. I weighed about 165 pounds; he was closer to 200 pounds and appeared to be in good physical shape as well. One day after having one of those arguments, he invited me to come to his house to fight him. I laughed at him and told him he was crazy. I then invited him to come to my house, which was in an all-Black neighborhood, to fight me. I think he got the message. When I had a concern on racial issues, I would go to Bob for answers. He normally would give me his honest opinion.

A carrier by the name of Gerald Cox had the best sense of humor of all the carriers in the office, and it was so much fun to be around him. There was never a dull moment when I was in his presence. I am not sure, but I always suspected that he had a customer play a practical joke on me one Saturday morning when I carried his route on his day off. As I was delivering the mail, I came upon a grandmotherly looking woman with gray hair, sitting on her front porch knitting. I walked up on the porch and said, "How are you doing, ma'am?" The little old lady politely stated that she was doing fine. She went on to tell me that she had read an article in the local newspaper indicating that the post office may close on Saturday and go to Monday-through-Friday delivery, which would likely result in layoffs for some workers. I verified that what she had said was true. She then stated, "I know what they ought to do." I fell right into the trap and asked, "What's that, ma'am?" and she replied, "They ought to lay those niggers off down there." I have been at a loss for words only a few times in my life, but this time was one I could clearly remember. As I walked off the porch, I glanced back, doing a double-take just to see if what I thought I had seen and heard had actually happened. As I looked back, I realized it had, and the little old gray-haired lady was still sitting there, smiling and rocking her chair as she continued to knit. I returned to the station and told a few select people about what happened and had a good laugh about it. I realized that I had grown as a person because I was able to tell some of my White acquaintances exactly what the lady had said to me and laugh with them about it.

I would be remiss if I did not speak about the dog encounters I had at Berry Street. What is a letter carrier without some good dog stories? I carried mail in a very nice neighborhood, and as I crossed the street to make my next delivery, something flashed across my line of vision. I soon realized that a huge dog had lunged at me, just barely missing me on the right side. The dog scared me so badly that the only thing I could think to do was to go on the offensive and attack the dog. I dropped my mailbag, balled my fist up, and went after it, flailing my fists and kicking my legs at the dog. It was surely fear that caused me to do such a dumb thing. I surprised myself with those tactics, but I believe I surprised the dog even more. To my relief, the dog tucked his tail and ran. He jumped the fence to go back where he had come from and continued to bark at me in a curious manner. I guess a human had never attacked him before, and judging by the look on the dog's face, he was probably wondering what kind of fool he had just encountered. One good thing did come out of that situation, though; I now had a strategy for dealing with dangerous attack dogs, or so I thought. I will explain later.

Another time while carrying mail I encountered a little white dog that charged at me every day on this route. I was not afraid of him, but he would pester me every day I carried the route. On this day, the dog got a little too close—or, should I say, he got close enough for me to kick him. The kick was one of those kicks anyone would be proud of. If I had been playing football, it would have been equivalent to kicking a field goal within the last few minutes to win the game. I hit that little dog perfectly. He went airborne, slammed against the side of the homeowner's garage, and slid down. It was a thing of beauty. I got a lot of satisfaction in that kick, but it did not stop the little dog from pestering me in the future. He was just smart enough, from that point on, to keep an appropriate distance, which just happened to be the length of my leg.

On one other occasion, violence almost occurred. I was walking toward a house to make a mail delivery when I noticed a large gray dog on the front porch and a little boy in the front yard. As any smart letter carrier would do, I asked the little boy if the dog would bite. He said no, so I proceeded up to the house to make my delivery. As I approached the dog, I patted him on the head and made my delivery. I turned around, stepped off the porch, and then felt an excruciating pain in my right hip. I knew what had happened. The dog had lived up to the stereotype about dogs and letter carriers. He had snuck up on me and bitten me on my buttocks. The violence I spoke of earlier is what almost happened because I wanted to hit that little boy for telling me the dog would not bite. But in retrospect, what did he know? I guess the dog had never bitten him. So I used my better judgment and hobbled on down the street with a slight limp and a hole in the back of my pants on the right side, probably with my underwear showing.

Another time, things happened so quickly that I had to just stand there in amazement, trying to figure out exactly what happened. I walked up on the porch to deliver the mail when a large German shepherd bolted out from behind the screen door, bit me on my wrist, and ran back into the house before the screen door closed. I stood there on the porch trying to figure out what the heck had just happened and looking at my wrist to determine whether the dog had broken my skin. The bite did hurt quite a bit and felt strong enough to break the skin, but fortunately it had not. It was a strange event, but I chalked it up as just another day in the life of a letter carrier.

While working at Berry Street Station, I found myself in a little trouble with management. It began when I failed to make a daily collection from a particular mailbox. The incident took place on the first day on my newly acquired route. I did not look at my route book prior to going out and did not know where my collection boxes were located. I came upon a mailbox that was on the corner of my route, which was adjacent to another route. I was not sure who was required to make the collection and concluded that it was another carrier's box, not mine to collect. The second day on the route, I realized the box was mine and began to collect mail from it daily.

Approximately one month later, the station manager walked up to me and presented me with a letter entitled "Letter of

Warning" and addressed to me. I was stunned. As I read the letter, I realized I was being charged with missing the collection box. My first reaction was that I had not missed the collection box in question, and I told my boss so. He instructed me to look at the date of the incident, which was cited in the warning letter. I soon realized it was referring to the incident about a month earlier. As I examined the letter more closely, I realized that the date just happened to be my first day back to work after being off for three weeks and after getting married to the prettiest girl in Stop Six, Texas (a comment said in front of me several years later by a couple of her classmates. I wish I had known that when I married her.). In addition, it was my first day carrying the route that I had bid on prior to going on vacation. Many firsts contributed to my missing the collection box, and I was very disappointed that, for a one-time mistake, I was issued a Letter of Warning. The letter also suggested I could be fired if I continued to have performance failures. I was so paranoid that I made small mistakes in fear of making big mistakes.

Included in the Letter of Warning was a mention of my right to talk to a manager in the personnel office to appeal or discuss the issue. Berry Street Station was a strong union station and well known for its union activism. The most radical union member at the station offered to assist me by accompanying me to the personnel office to discuss the letter. I told him that if I allowed him to accompany me, he would get both of us fired. I spoke to the personnel manager alone, and we had a very good meeting. As time passed, the Letter of Warning was expunged from my file.

As time moved on, very few race-related remarks were made as openly as they had been in my first few months at Berry Street

Station, but there were some difficult and very challenging days ahead. Early in my employment there, I was assigned to a route next to a letter carrier named Asa Phelps. Asa was an outspoken segregationist but avoided making openly racist comments, at least in front of me. However, one day we got into a conversation about Angela Davis, a Black activist who had ties with the Black Panthers. Asa was really bad-mouthing Angela, especially since she had just announced her loyalty to the Communist Party. I maintained my cool but offered my thoughts about her and the Communist Party announcement. You must realize that this was 1968, and there were still growing pains in race relations and in any workplace where Whites and Blacks were working side by side, for the first time in many cases. I told Asa that Angela Davis more than likely chose to be a Communist because she felt Communism possibly offered Blacks the best opportunity to achieve equality in this country at that time. He looked at me and said plainly, "You're dumb." I was very cool, and I calmly asked him what he had said. He repeated himself. He probably thought I would attack him, and I did think about it but also knew two things. First, I needed my job, and second, I needed to be smarter than that. I also needed to do something he least expected, and that was to outthink him. Therefore, I asked him several questions, beginning with whether he had been White all his life. He did not have a clue to where I was going with that question, which was just fine with me. He asked me what that had to do with anything. I told him to just answer my question, and he stated that he had. I asked him that if he had received all the privileges and opportunities provided to and for White people in this country. He answered yes. I asked him if he had he attended college, and he answered that he had for two years.

Then I wanted to address his statement about my being dumb. I began by telling him that I grew up in a segregated society and attended segregated schools. I also made him aware that, all my life, I had heard White people proclaim that Blacks were inferior to them, Blacks schools were inferior to White schools, Black teachers were inferior to White teachers, and that Blacks were in general inferior to Whites in all respects. I went on to tell him that I attended those so-called inferior schools, had those so-called inferior teachers, and had only a high school education. I explained to him that, in this country, I was treated as a second-class citizen, and as such, I had to overcome all kinds of hurdles that he did not. I stated that I had taken and passed the same employment test that he had, that I was working on the same job as he was, that I was performing the same work as he was, and that I was receiving pay comparable to his. Then I threw him the question he was not prepared to answer. I asked him, "Now, with all those roadblocks that prevented me from enjoying the same privileges that you had as a White person in this country and with the fact that I am standing right next to you doing the same job as you are, who did you say was dumb?" Asa Phelps did not appreciate what had just happened to him, but I did shut him up. He did not say anything else derogatory to me.

As time passed, things did not get any better at Berry Street and in fact got worse. Racial insensitivity was common at the station. Berry Street Station was known around town as a strong union station, with strong city representation. Someone there decided to put my name in for station shop steward. I did not know much about the union, and I even thought a Black organization named the Alliance was part of the Letter Carrier

Union. I was aware of one other Black letter carrier, who just happened to be a friend of my father's. He was an officer in the Alliance, and I did not realize that it was not the Letter Carrier or Postal Union. I later found out that Blacks, for a long period, were not welcome in the all-White postal unions, so Black employees formed what was called the Alliance, which included not only Black postal workers but also Blacks from other federal agencies. However, in 1967, the union was integrated, and Blacks could join the Postal Service Union, even though most Blacks still belonged to the Alliance and did not trust they would get proper representation in postal unions. Three candidates were in contention for the shop steward position at Berry Street, and I initially believed my name was placed in the mix as a joke.

Some old-timers at the station began making racist remarks after learning that my name was included on the list of candidates. Based on how they were reacting, I decided to keep my name in the mix. The voting was completed, and to my surprise, I got the second highest number of votes, but none of us got over 50 percent. Therefore, a runoff was required, and that was when things really got ugly. The racist remarks were flying. However, no one said anything racist to me personally. I went to my old friend, Bob Young, and asked him why some felt it necessary to resort to racist remarks. He seemed somewhat perplexed. I knew in my heart that it was possible that, at some other time, he himself might have been right in the middle of the racist remarks. My plan was to put this situation on his mind because I truly felt he liked me for some reason and was not party to the remarks. I was not sure whether he was or was not a bigot, but I trusted he was not. His reaction to my question reassured me that he was probably not making any of the remarks. He told me he really did not know why they were being made and assured me they should not have been part of the process.

I lost the election, which was no surprise to me, but my feelings about working at Berry Street Station began to sour. My relationship with some of the White carriers changed, and I became more sensitive to comments being made around the office. In addition, other pressures were also beginning to take a toll on me. The year was now 1972, and there were issues all over the city related to race relations and race issues. During that time, a Black organization operated in town that called themselves the United Front. They demonstrated around the city and received quite a bit of TV coverage. Their demonstrations had an impact on how all my White customers dealt with me. They did not treat me any differently, but they did ask me about the demonstrations and what I thought about those "colored boys." I could not speak as freely as I would have liked, and that created some anxiety problems for me. As time rocked on, I became more and more agitated by what was happening in the office as well as what was going on in the community. I knew I had to decide on my future as a letter carrier or truly "go postal" if I remained at Berry Street Station. I made a smart decision to put in a bid to be moved to an area of town where I knew I would not encounter the same problems I was facing at Berry Street.

# Chapter 8

## Second Stage of Going Postal

I bid on a route in an area of town that was predominantly Black and with a station where almost half the carriers were Black. I thought that going to the Southtown Annex Station would mean I would no longer have to deal with racist remarks in the office or on the street. Prior to leaving Berry Street, I informed some of the carriers working with me of my decision to leave and in what part of town I would be working. Something that happened perplexed me then, and I remain perplexed to this date. A person working next to me who, for all practical purposes did not care much for me or Black people, made an interesting remark. He told me I should not have bid on that route. He said that the area was crime ridden and that I would not be safe carrying mail in that neighborhood. I did not know whether he was genuinely concerned about my well-being or just that scared of the Black community. What he said did not change my mind. I concluded that I knew my people a lot better than he did, and I felt I could deal with whatever that area dealt me.

I did, however, hear rumors about letter carriers being beat up and threatened on the route that I had bid for. I also heard stories, which were not rumors, of a carrier being hit in the head with a hammer when he did not give a customer his social security check. Another story told of a letter carrier who went into an establishment on the corner of Evans and Rosedale, which just happened to be the toughest area of town, and was caught up in a robbery.

As the story goes, the carrier entered the establishment, which was also a gambling den, and found himself in the middle of gunplay. the gunman was part of a dice game, and there was some kind of misunderstanding. The gunman stepped outside and then reentered the establishment after the carrier had gone in to deliver the mail. The gunman ordered everyone to raise their hands and get against the wall. The carrier threw his hands up and then said, "Mister, does that include me?" According to the story, the gunman did not realize the carrier had come in and told him to get his fat ass out of there. The carrier in question was about six foot four and weighed over three hundred pounds. In fact, this carrier is the one who told the story about the events of that day. After I reported to Southtown Annex, this carrier told me another story that I will share later.

As I began my work at Southtown Annex, I learned that it was not a full-service station, did not offer sales to the public, and only housed letter carriers, with a small clerk operation to support the carrier operation. While there I realized several things. The workforce was somewhat different from what I had expected, and the route that I had bid on was even more interesting than the stories that were previously told me.

While working at Southtown, I encountered the same racist attitudes that I had previously encountered at Berry Street, but they were not as overt. The White carriers at Southtown would openly speak their minds about the things they believed in, while the Black carriers were kind of passive and would not challenge what the White carriers were saying and doing in the office.

I went to Southtown Station with a chip on my shoulder, and I was determined that I would not go through the same things I had at Berry Street. I soon began to challenge White carriers at every turn and quickly developed a reputation. We had open dialogue on race relations in the country, and I offered my opinion on all issues. The supervisors also developed a biased opinion of me, based on my not being shy about speaking my mind. That opinion was mainly based on my outspokenness and what they perceived as an angry young Black man or militant, as we were called back then. There were a lot of angry Black men and women during this period of race relations, mainly because of the Civil Rights Movement and serving in the military. The whole system was designed for Blacks to serve in places like Vietnam, but once we returned home from that service, we had limited rights as American citizens. The significance of the Vietnam era was that Black men were drafted into the military in disproportionately higher numbers than Whites, and after being drafted, they were placed on the front lines and took the brunt of the action and number of casualties, as well. This was a time when Black men were not willing to make that kind of sacrifice, as did those during WWII and the Korean conflict, and not demand their rights once back in the States or returning home from the armed services. This was not a time to be passive about anything but to be passionate about one's beliefs. I was very passionate about my beliefs and my place and time in this country, and I was determined to have a voice. I worked with one mean-spirited person at Southtown Annex who always had something negative to say about the Black people on the route where he delivered. He would talk about how bad their houses smelled and how dirty the children and the people were. He may have been stating the truth, but I was tired of hearing what he had to say, especially about Black people and especially because his comments seemed to be racially motivated. After hearing all I cared to hear of his complaints, I told him a story about my making a choice when I left Berry Street Station. I told him that I did not like working there because of some of the people on my route and some of the carriers in the office. I told him of my decision to leave that station and go to another one where I would feel more comfortable. Then I lowered the boom on him. I told him that if he felt the way he did about carrying mail in Black neighborhoods, he should do as I did—use his seniority and bid to move to an area of town that was more appealing to him. I told him he should bid to an area where Black folks did not live. I had done exactly that by leaving the all-White community where I was carrying mail. He did not make another comment, at least not in front of me, about the Black folks on his route. He also did not take my advice but remained on the route. I thought I had him under control, but his mean-spirited behavior would surface once again.

We had a new carrier who reported for duty at Southtown Annex. His parents lived across the street from a fellow carrier in the office, and I soon found out that he was the younger brother of a former classmate of mine. We accepted him with open arms since we had a sense of knowing him. He was quite a character, but as with most newly appointed carriers, he had a lot to learn about delivering mail. After returning to the station after delivering the route to which he was assigned, this same old carrier, who was working on the adjacent route, noticed the young carrier had failed to deliver a small amount of the mail that should have been delivered on the route. The old carrier, I guess, felt some ownership of the route, or maybe he was looking out for the carrier who was off that day. He questioned the young carrier about the mail he did not deliver. His intent was fine, but the way he was questioning this young carrier caused me concern; I felt he was talking to him the way White people talked to Black people during the Jim Crow period, from which were not too far removed, if at all. He was speaking to him in a belittling and very demeaning tone. I took all I could take and jumped right into the fracas. I walked over to the older carrier, and I challenged him. I asked if he was the younger carrier's supervisor, and he said no. I then told him that he did not have a damn thing to say to him. As you can tell, I was angry, and I was not going to allow the clock to be turned back regarding how White people treated and talked to Black people, at least not in my presence. I decided that, after living in New York City and Los Angeles and then serving in the US Army, I would not sit idly by and allow those old racist attitudes go unchallenged as we had been required to in the past. I had gotten the older carrier's attention, and he left the younger one alone. I do not recall having any more problems with that older White carrier.

The office was full of older White carriers who had begun their careers when Blacks were not allowed to work at the post office. One older White carrier was the senior carrier in the office and a person for whom most everyone in the office had respect and would listen to, even the Black carriers. He did have some old-fashioned beliefs and sometimes would display a lack of respect for Black folks. On one morning, a Black carrier who lived in the Stop Six area of town, where I resided as well, was discussing the new Dairy Queen fast-food restaurant that was going to be built in our neighborhood. It was a big deal to us because we did not have any businesses like that in Black neighborhoods. The older White carrier had been listening and stated, "I don't know why they are building a Dairy Queen in that area" and then added, "All those people out there are going to do is tear it up." His comments infuriated me, and I challenged him and asked him how the hell he would know what "those people" would do one way or the other. I considered his comment offensive, demeaning, and stereotypical of what White folks thought of Black folks. He tried to explain what he meant by his statement, but I told him I had heard him clearly and then shared what I thought about what he said. I also told him I did not want to hear anything else about the subject. He left me alone and walked out of the aisle.

This was new territory for just about anybody who worked at Southtown Annex. No one had ever told this older carrier off or challenged him as I did. No one said a word during our encounter. As the older White carrier left the aisle and went to the restroom, one of the older Black carriers, whom I truly loved, walked over to me and said, "That's what I like about you." He stated that he liked the fact that I would not back down from the White carriers. He told me this while the White carrier was not nearby, and as soon as the older White carrier came back in the aisle, the older Black carrier rushed back to his workstation as if he had never spoken to me. This was very typical of the older Black carriers; they avoided confrontation with the White carriers and put up with almost anything they said. However, I was not so naive that I did not understand this was how older

Black men had survived Jim Crow. They took things I would not take, but they paved the way for me to bring my attitude to the new day. Thanks to them all.

Just for the record, the Dairy Queen was one of the first chain establishments built in our Black neighborhood, and we—that is, some of us—were very proud to have such an establishment in the neighborhood. Unfortunately, many years later, the Black people in the area did just as the older White carrier had said; they tore the place up, and the company closed the business. As a people, we still had a way to go, it seemed. At the time the Dairy Queen closed, I was glad I no longer worked at Southtown Station because I know I would have heard, "I told you so."

Southtown Annex was a great place for a young Black carrier to work. We had many political and world-events discussions in the office. There was never a dull moment. I recall having a discussion about race relations with a carrier working next to me. He told me that he had a right to be a bigot if he wanted to. I responded that he was right; however, if his bigotry interfered with my rights as a US citizen, then his bigotry was wrong. I told him he could be whatever he wanted to be at home, but once he had to interact with people outside his home, that was another story. He seemed to be somewhat surprised about what I said, but he did not disagree with me.

As time passed, I developed a reputation as a militant, outspoken, angry, young Black male. I would challenge anyone in the office who said the slightest thing that resembled a racist remark. As a matter of fact, I was always talking back to the other carriers when the manager or one of the supervisors would walk by, and they would only hear my comments but not what had set me off. It was like a football player who retaliates for an illegal hit but the referee only sees his retaliation and not the initial foul. To reinforce what the managers at Southtown thought about me, I stupidly snapped at the station manager one day. For a little background information, there was one Black carrier who had almost everyone in the office fearful of him. He stood about six foot three and was an imposing figure. It appeared that he always got his way with just about everything. He would ask for assistance on his route, indicating that he could not carry it in the allotted time. I had no clue about how the supervisors made the determination to assist someone at the time, and it seemed to me that this carrier was too lazy to do his own work. One day the station manager came over to my workstation and made a mistake. Normally, the manager would tell a carrier what he wanted him or her to do rather than asking for what he wanted. On that day, the manager asked me if I would carry what we called swings off this letter carrier. Before I knew it, I had said, "Hell, no." However, I quickly realized what I had said and knew I had to clean it up, especially after noticing the way he looked at me. I then told him that if he was asking me, I did not want to carry the other carrier's mail; however, if he was instructing me, I would. He again gave me a funny look and walked off without requiring me to carry the swings. That was not a good day for me. And it would possibly come back to haunt me another day.

After reporting to Southtown and carrying the route I was assigned, I soon realized that the area of town was everything I had heard it was and possibly more. The route was located right in the middle of the most notorious red-light district in Fort Worth. Initially I enjoyed every minute of it. I became, in many people's eyes, somewhat of a celebrity. Everyone wanted to talk to the mailman. This was the early seventies, and hair was the thing. I had a huge afro and a huge mustache. The average dopehead or dope pusher looked just like me minus the postal uniform. Many people on the street really believed I had drugs for sale in my mail pouch, and I was often asked for them.

Some people who drove up and down the main drag, Evans Avenue, would wave at me as if I were someone special and not just the mailman. In fact, one person who drove the drag quite often was an insurance salesman. One night while attending a party, I just happened to run into him. He looked at me and said, "You're that mailman." I was out of uniform, but he recognized me. He told me to go with him, and I asked him what he wanted. He replied that he had some "dynamite drugs" he wanted to share with me, which turned out to be marijuana. I did something that really burst his bubble: I told him I did not smoke marijuana, and I could just see the disappointment on his face. He could not believe what I was saying, especially given the way I looked. The mustache and the "fro" conveyed that I was hip and a worldly street person. I lost my celebrity status with him, and he no longer waved at me as he drove by.

I was still popular with most of the people on the route, however. On one bright Saturday morning, the streets were loaded with people standing around on the corners, which was normal for this area of town. However, I encountered a problem that I was not sure how to handle. A big guy who appeared to be a druggie and had a reputation as a violent person on the streets approached me and asked for five dollars. I did not want to give it to him because I knew that, if I did, I would never get rid of him. He was not someone I could say no to, however. He appeared to be every bit as dangerous as his reputation suggested. I had to make a quick decision, and I opted to give him the five dollars, hoping that would be the end of it. I hoped.

Strangely enough, I did not see him for several weeks. I assumed he did not want to see me since he owed me money. How wrong I was. On another Saturday morning I noticed him standing with a group of guys on the corner. My first inclination was to turn around and go the other way, hoping he did not see me. But I was out of luck—he had seen me. He began walking quickly toward me. I knew I was in trouble, and I knew I had to stop this madness because I could not continue giving him my money. My mama did not raise no fool, as the old saying goes. As he was approaching me, I began walking even faster toward him. He got the strangest look on his face, apparently totally confused. When I reached him, and before he could say anything to me, I asked him, "Do you have any money?" I was smart enough not to ask for my money. I told him I was broke and needed to borrow some money from him. He was caught totally off guard. He told me that he did not have any. Guess what? I never saw him again after that encounter. It surely pays to think on your feet, and I got away with one that day.

The route I had taken on was full of colorful people as well as that one barbershop that always seems to be the focal point or gathering point for some of those characters. I hung out at the barbershop to hear the latest neighborhood news and the latest funny stories. I even started getting my hair cut there after I found a barber I felt comfortable with.

There were also colorful individuals working at Southtown as well. I previously mentioned this very large letter carrier who had worked my route before I took it. He had a huge weakness:

he loved Black women and fraternized with the local prostitutes. One morning, he came to me and said, "They got me." I asked him what he was speaking of, and he explained that, on the previous payday, he had picked up a prostitute and gone to a local motel. He then made a fatal error. He said he got out his pants and left them on the chair as he went to the restroom. The prostitute took his pants with his billfold in the pocket, and the billfold contained money from his payroll check that he had just cashed. When he walked out of the bathroom, the prostitute was gone, as were his pants. He had to call a friend to bring him pants. At first, I did not believe him, but the more he talked, I began to somewhat believe him. When I went out on the route that day, I got confirmation that the story was true. One of those colorful individuals I spoke of earlier was running a small club on the strip. He came out as he saw me walking down the street and asked if I had heard the latest. I asked him what he was talking about, and he told me that a prostitute had robbed the big redheaded carrier. He verified that the prostitute had taken the carrier's pants and billfold and then put his billfold in the mailbox on the corner. His comments confirmed what the big redhead had told me back at the office. Now that was something to live down, but the big redhead seemed to wear this misfortunate incident as a badge of honor.

One night as I was leaving the barbershop with my boys and wife, the club owner I just spoke of flagged me down. What happened next was related to the image I had cultivated on the street while carrying mail—that of a streetwise drug user or dealer. As he flagged me down, I knew I needed to get out of the car because I was not sure what that fool was going to say to me, especially in front my wife. As I got out of the car, he told me that he had some pills he needed to move, and he needed my assistance. Can you believe he was talking about my assisting him in a drug deal? That cultivated image had come back to haunt me big time. The situation called for some fast thinking, again. I had to come up with something quick to deal with the unfortunate situation I had gotten myself in, and at the same time, I had the problem of trying to maintain my well-cultivated image. That image was about survival in this very tough neighborhood. Therefore, I verbally assaulted him. I went into a very aggressive mode and began to curse him. I told him, "You dumb m-----f-----! I don't do business when I'm with my wife and family!" The guy backed up and stammered, "I'm sorry. I did not know that was your wife. I thought that was your hoe." That exchange was okay with me, especially since it got me off the hook. When I got back into the car, I told my wife what had transpired, and all she could do was laugh. I was so happy that she had a good sense of humor about it. I also explained to her that most of the people on the street thought I was a lot more than just the mailman. I mentioned a mailbox on the corner previously. On any given Monday morning, when I went to collect the mail, I would also retrieve many billfolds that belonged to the various men who frequented the local "businesswomen" over the weekend. The businesswomen would allow the billfolds to be returned to their owners, absent, of course, any cash. I got to know one of the local prostitutes fairly well. She was very pretty woman. She was tall, dark, and what the brothers of my day called "slender fine." I loaned her money from time to time, and she always promised to repay me. No, not with what you may be thinking—she repaid me the money I loaned her. I questioned her about why she chose to be a prostitute, and she tried to explain. I told her that, with her looks and what appeared to be normal intelligence, she did not have to sell her body. I later found out that many of the women of the night became prostitutes to pay for their drug addictions, and in many cases, their pimps were also their drug dealers. I was not sure this was the case with this young woman, but it probably was. What else could explain why this desirable woman was prostituting herself? As a rule, I did not frequent that area during the evening hours, but on any given evening, ladies of the night were on the street, including my friend, all dressed up and peddling their goods. What a shame and a waste, especially in relation to that beautiful woman. However, that's life.

There was always something going on inside and outside the post office. I did some very dumb things due to my naivete. During one holiday season at Southtown Annex, I walked into the post office with a glass of liquor someone had given me on my route in the spirit of Christmas cheer. One of the senior carriers asked me about it and whether I was looking to be fired for bringing liquor on the job. I told him it was Christmas and that it had seemed to be okay when I was at Berry Street. He said it was not okay and told me to get rid of it. I truly respected him and did what he told me. I did not realize how much trouble I could have gotten myself into. On another occasion, the supervisor gave me baby diapers that were undeliverable and would be thrown away. I did not know if the supervisor knew better or not, but I learned later that postal employees were prohibited from taking any mail, including throw-away mail, from the post office.

The Southtown area could be referred to as the hood, as my boys would call it, or the ghetto, as e said in my day. As I was carrying mail one day, I encountered my second vicious dog. Every day that I went by this house, I heard a dog cutting up something awful in the backyard behind a very tall wooden fence, as if he was trying to get to me as I was walking by. I always thought that it was a good thing the dog was behind a fence because he sounded so vicious. My greatest fear came to bear, however. One Saturday as I was approaching the house, I noticed that the dog was out, and he did not waste any time coming after me. I remembered the formula I had developed a few years earlier. As the dog charged, I dropped my mail bag, balled up my fists, and went into attack mode, flailing my arms and legs at the dog. There was one problem—the dog did not back off. I had not taken into consideration that this dog was raised in a different neighborhood, and he clearly did not respect my formula for dog fighting that I had developed for a different kind of dog in a more affluent neighborhood. I believe I heard the dog say, "That shit won't work in this neighborhood!" The incident was getting scary, and I did everything I could think of, but nothing seemed to work. I just knew I was going to be ripped apart. We went around and around in the street, and I was getting tired. Fortunately, I saw a large rock on the side of the street and was able to get to it before the dog could get to me. I picked up the rock and threw it at the dog, just barely hitting him across the head, but it was just hard enough to hurt him and cause him to back off. He ran back to his yard. That was the end of my dog-fighting days. I started carrying a big stick instead.

As time rocked on at Southtown, however, I got more and more angry. I found fault with my supervisors and with most of the people in the office. I would argue with anyone who differed with me. I was truly on the road to self-destruction. Daily, I woke up angry at the world and just looking for a fight. Supervisors stayed away from me unless contact was absolutely necessary. My friends were suspicious of me, wondering about my temper and afraid I was a time bomb just waiting to explode. I hated going to work and did not trust anyone in management.

Part of my distrust for the station management began when my grandfather died in 1973. I had previously lost both of my parents and had grown very close to my grandparents. My grandmother, knowing I was out on my route carrying mail, called my wife at her job and told her my grandfather had died. My wife in turn called my station manager and advised him of my grandfather's death in hopes that he would contact me on the route. I carried mail down the side of the freeway, and as I was walking the route, my wife, who was being driven by her supervisor, noticed me. They exited the freeway and drove down the access road to get to me. My wife asked me, "What are you doing out here?"

I said, "Delivering mail."

I asked her what she was doing out on my route, and she asked, "Didn't you hear?"

"Hear what?"

She replied, "Your grandfather died."

It hit me like a ton of bricks. My grandfather, in his midseventies, was a picture of health, and his death was the last thing I expected.

My wife told me that she had called my manager an hour earlier and made him aware, and I became very angry. I went to my vehicle and headed back to the post office. I was so angry at my station manager for not notifying and relieving me that I knew it was in my best interest not to say anything to my him because I would have said something I would later regret. When I got to the station, I mumbled under my breath that I could not believe he had not notified me that my grandfather had died. I went in and clocked out. My wife and I proceeded to my grandmother's house on the north part of town. Under normal circumstances, I probably would have returned to work the next day, but I decided I would not return until after the funeral. I called the station and talked to a good friend of mine who acted as an intermediary for me. He spoke to the manager about my absence and made him aware of how upset I was. I also told my friend that if the manager tried to do anything about my time off, I would go to the postmaster and enlighten him to what had taken place.

I reported to work about a week later, still angry. I was just waiting for the manager to say something to me about my absence so I could tell him what I really had on my mind. He never said a word. However, that did not help what I thought about him and his management style. I saw him as a petty, narrow-minded person. Every decision he made I thought was wrong. I hated going to work, and dealing with him daily was a major chore.

I soon began to get bored carrying mail and decided to go to trade school or college to qualify myself for advancement. I initially applied with a training institute called Electronic Data. I took the entrance exam required to begin training as an electronic technician, in which I would learn how to repair the new electronic equipment that the Postal Service was installing. After passing the exam, I was going to have to travel to Dallas five nights a week to attend class. I decided that I did not want to drive back to Fort Worth at ten o'clock every night, so I decided to take some college courses instead.

I entered a local junior college and took up accounting. I knew the Postal Service had an accounting department and figured I could land a job there.

Starting college began a new chapter in my life. I took classes in sociology and psychology, and the sociology classes had the greatest impact on me. While working at Southtown Annex, I had alienated the management staff because of my very aggressive behavior. The sociology course opened my eyes to the issues that Black people were dealing with during the turbulent decade of the seventies and how those issues ultimately influenced my behavior. I began seeing people differently, especially those of different races and cultures. I began to understand myself better and learned to be more tolerant of people who had different beliefs, looked different, and acted differently than me. I even saw the management team differently, and it was no longer a chore to go to work as it once was.

However, my previous poor attitude was about to come back to haunt me. When I started getting bored with carrying mail, I had bid on what we called a T-6 route, which consisted of carrying five different routes during the week. I reasoned that would break the monotony of carrying the same route and seeing the same people everyday. That helped a little, but I needed more.

I had taken several supervisory examinations in an attempt to break into management. The station manager notified me that some higher-ups were interested in me for a position at the main office. He told me that he had to make a recommendation but first needed to interview me. My world was just about to end, or so it seemed. This was a person I had alienated and detested most of the time I worked for him, and he was now in charge of deciding my future. I was in trouble, and I knew it. This was the same manager who had asked me a few weeks earlier to carry mail off another carrier, and I had told him "Hell, no." How would I deal with this situation? How could I dig myself out of this humongous hole I had dug for myself?

As in previous situations where I had to make quick decisions, when my manager called me in for the interview, I had to quickly come up with something to change his mind about me. I knew what he thought about me just from reading his body language. Before he could start his question-and-answer session, I aggressively told him that he was not equipped to make a recommendation because he did not know anything about me. He looked at me as if to say, *What the hell is he talking about now?* But I did not let him talk. I went on to tell him who Willie Hargis really was.

I told him about my view of life, and I emphasized my newly developed understanding of human relations and race relations. Whatever I told him—and I am not completely sure what all I said—but it worked. My manager said one thing to me that caught me off guard. He told me he thought I was a racist. His choice of words surprised me because I did not see a Black person who may or may not have liked White people as racist. My understanding of racism was a situation in which someone who had power over someone else used that power to disadvantage the other. I told him that I was not a racist, explained to him that I disagreed with many racist remarks that others were making at work, and told him that the problem was that he would always see me retaliating for those remarks when he had not heard what the other person said. I added that I was not a person who would hear people make racist comments, stand idle, and not respond. I explained that I was outspoken but did not harbor any dislike for any group of people. I guess he took me at my word; he recommended me for the job.

At other times, I really enjoyed working at Southtown Annex. I met one man who inspired me to be a better person and try to accomplish my goals. I had the utmost respect for him, and he advised me on buying my first and last home. I was a little concerned about taking on the expense of a mortgage, but he encouraged me to buy the house and assured me that my house note would basically remain the same while I would continue to receive pay increases throughout my postal career. His advice was profound, and it worked just as he stated.

There were others in the station with whom I developed a great relationship and I will always remember. I was reunited with the carrier with whom I had begun my career, Van Malone, and we continued our relationship for many years to come. Another older carrier whom I called Pops because he reminded me of my father became an inspiration to me as well. He was probably the sharpest-dressing carrier in the unit. He always had on a starched shirt, pressed pants, and polished shoes, even after returning from his route on a hot summer day. I could not figure out how he did that. A friend of mine shared that he kept fresh uniforms in one of the office buildings on his route where he delivered mail, and he would change clothes prior to returning to the office. He was one of my favorites.

Lyon Fields was another carrier with whom I developed a great relationship and who always had profound things to say. He was a big guy, standing about six foot three or four. Our relationship flourished, and I could say almost anything to him. On several occasions, I noticed that he had a very short temper and would fight or at least let people know he was not afraid of physical confrontation. One time, he reacted this way when a carrier moved his lunch to another table in order to use the table to play dominoes. He became very upset, and I really thought he was going to attack the other carriers for touching his sack lunch. It got a little ugly. On another day, we were processing Jet and Ebony magazines for delivery, and I asked him if he read them. He responded that he did not read that junk. Well, for those who do not know, these magazines kept Black people in touch with the latest information in the Black community across the United States, and they were the leading Black magazines at the time. Knowing the significance of the magazines in America, I was somewhat surprised by his answer, especially calling the magazines junk. I told him that he was the blackest White man I had ever met, which got a laugh from all the carriers working alongside us, including some of the White carriers. He also found my comments funny. That was a great relationship that flourished for years, and when he decided to get married again, he asked me to be his best man. In addition, during the period of our great relationship, he would visit my home and I would visit his. He got to know my wife and my two boys. My wife became pregnant with our third and youngest son, and I informed my coworkers. All the carriers congratulated me; however, this good friend of mine had something a little more colorful to say. He was dark complected, and he told me that the baby my wife was carrying was actually his. Now you know we had a great relationship because not many people would have the guts to tell another man anything like that. He was waiting on my response, and I did not disappoint him. I quickly replied that the baby could be my wife's color (very light) or my color (brown), but if the baby was one ounce darker than me, I was going to whip his big black (very dark) ass. That got a great laugh from him and the others who overheard our conversation. What a relationship.

Even though a couple of the carriers at Southtown Annex harbored racist attitudes, I found myself truly liking them. They were fun to be around, and from time to time, each would say things that would rub me the wrong way, but I never fell out with them. One carrier took pride in letting me know that he was of German heritage, as if to say Germans were the superior race. I always countered that he was closer to being a German shepherd than a German. He would laugh at my comment, not necessarily offended. We had a good relationship. I will discuss the other carrier later.

Many people I met on the route had lasting impressions on me. One older Black man gave me some advice one day that I have thought of and used over the years; it was life changing. I was having difficulties with a good friend, and I let the situation affect me. The old man told me, and I quote, "Have more and more friends, and need them less and less." I initially did not know what the heck he meant by that, but I acted as if I did. As I walked down the street, I thought about it, trying to figure out what he really meant. It soon dawned on me, and I realized how profound his words were. He was telling me that my world was too small and I needed to broaden my horizons. He was saying that, if I had more friends, I would not be so bothered by the actions of one. I would not miss the relationship with that one person because I would have many others to fill the void. These were great words from an older Black male, whom I suspect had very little formal education but had good advice for a young man finding his way through life.

There was another older Black man who shared a little wisdom with me. As we were talking one day, he told me about a White coworker of his at the packing house. This person came by his house one day and was surprised at how well he was living. The White person asked him how he was able to afford all the nice things he had, and he replied that they both worked at the same plant and made about the same salary—and then lowered the boom. He told his coworker that he (the Black man) must have been smarter than he (the White man) was and knew how to manage his money better. He said he resented the man's asking him about how he was living, and that's why he said what he did.

I had a strange experience with an older lady on my route with whom I had developed a friendly relationship. One day, a man drove a truck down one of my delivery streets and was selling fresh vegetables. The woman stopped the man to buy sweet potatoes and other vegetables. She told me that I needed to buy some sweet potatoes too so my wife could cook me a sweet potato pie. I replied that my wife did not know how to cook a sweet potato pie, so she said she would cook one for me. I thought that was so nice of her, and I bought a batch of potatoes and gave them to her. A day or so later, she told me that she had my pie ready. She invited me into her house to get it. At first, I did not want to go in because it was against regulations, but I figured she was an old woman and I would be in her house for just a few minutes, so I went in. If she had brought it out to me, I would not have seen what I saw. When she went to her refrigerator to take the pie out, I saw something unexpected. She opened the refrigerator door, and I saw critters crawling inside the refrigerator. I was shocked at what I saw, but I did not let on. I thanked her for the pie, not saying anything about what I had seen, and took it back to my mail vehicle. After leaving the street, I threw the pie in the first garbage can I saw. I was so glad I had broken the rules and gone inside the house. I had assumed she was clean and had a clean house, so I would have eaten the pie. Whew!

When I first began carrying mail on the south side of town, I learned a lesson in customer service and customer satisfaction. A White woman who lived in my delivery area was notorious for chewing out letter carriers for the slightest mistake. I was aware of her and how she treated letter carriers, so I set out to do a good job and try to get on her good side. After several days of delivering that portion of my route, I realized that she enjoyed working in her yard and her flower bed. I had this bright idea to try to connect with her by commenting on her lawn. I told her she had a beautiful lawn and commented on how hard she worked in her yard. Believe it or not, we developed a great relationship just because I had made that comment. In fact, I misdelivered a letter to her residence one day, which was not uncommon for a letter carrier to do every once in a while, and the next day she told me that I needed to speak with the substitute carrier she believed had worked my route the previous day about misdelivering mail to her residence. I was not about to tell her that it was in fact me who had done it. We continued to have a great relationship while I delivered mail to that area.

I also met the criminal element on my route, and I developed relationships with real criminals and people who had spent time in prison. The relations did not go far, but they enjoyed talking with me and I was able to speak their language, which kept me safe. I built a relationship with one man who had been recently released from prison, and in our conversations, he said that he had learned landscaping while in prison. I had recently moved to a new neighborhood and my lawn needed work, so I picked him up on a few afternoons and had him work on my lawn. I did not think about any possible consequences of that decision, but fortunately, he did only what I requested of him and never caused me any problems.

Time passed, and there was no word on whether I would receive the promotion I was seeking. I lost a large portion of the route I had been carrying due to route adjustments, and I decided it was time to move on. I had always wanted to work out of the station that was in the part of town where I lived for two reasons. First, most of the delivery area consisted of nice neighborhoods, and second, if I had to, I could walk to work. I was less than three miles from my home. I placed a bid for what was called a T-6 position at the Glencrest Station, where I would carry a different route each day, and was awarded the bid. I began working there and quickly started thinking about the routes I could bid on in next cycle that would place me closer to my house and in better neighborhoods. As I recall, I was the second-most senior person in the T-6 group, so I had the luxury of bidding on some very good routes.

However, less than a month after reporting to Glencrest Station, I was called to the main office to interview for the position I had previously applied for. I had almost forgotten about the job.

It was a building service supervisor position. The job duties were to supervise the cleaning services at the main post office. Some of my acquaintances told me that if I took the job, I would be a glorified janitor. I did not think of it like that, though; I saw it as an opportunity to get my foot in the door of management.

I met with the Maintenance manager for the interview. The interview went well, but he asked one question that I was not sure I answered the way he expected me to. He asked me if I was prejudiced, and I immediately stated that I was. He seemed to be totally unprepared for that answer. Now, as I have stated time and time again, my mother did not raise no fool. I quickly added that I had many prejudices, but if he was referring to racial prejudices, then no, I was not racially prejudiced. I could see the relief on his face. I knew exactly what he was seeking when he asked the question, but I guess I had a little bit of smart ass in me and played a little mind game with him. It was obvious the manager had not posed the question correctly, and I guess I was not above letting him know. It was a calculated risk, and it could have backfired on me. Fortunately, it worked, and I was selected for the position.

# Chapter 9

## Third Stage of Going Postal

As I said, I started taking college courses in January 1973 while carrying mail at Southtown Annex. By the time I was promoted to building service supervisor in 1975, I had completed about two years of college work at Tarrant County Junior College. The building service supervisor position was the lowest-level supervisory position in the Postal Service. I was assigned to the evening shift at the main post office, which worked perfectly for me in conjunction with my pursuit of a college education. For the record, the Post Office has three shifts, which are called tours. Tour 1 was the all-night shift; Tour 2 was the day shift; and Tour 3 was the evening shift. About the same time as my promotion, it became necessary for me to move on to a four-year college, and because I was assigned to the evening shift, I was able to enter Texas Wesleyan College and take day courses. Working evenings also benefited me in other ways as well. I was basically unsupervised during the evening shift and once I got my crew assigned to their work areas, I could go back to my office and do my homework. I had one problem with that, however. One evening when I was doing my homework, I was confronted by the tour 3 superintendent, who had a reputation of being one of the meanest managers in mail processing. He was concerned about a problem on the floor and came down to the Maintenance area looking for me. Because there were no Maintenance managers on tour 3, this manager was effectively my manager. When he got to my office, I had books spread all over the place, as I was deep into my homework. I just knew my short tenure as a supervisor was about to end. To my surprise, the superintendent did not mention anything about what he saw and just had me address the problem on the floor. Later I learned something very important about the manager that I will address later.

My new job was uneventful, but I had to dust off some skills I had learned in various leadership positions I had held going back to my high school days as commander of my NDCC/ROTC unit and as a platoon guide in basic training. Some had the school of thought that supervising cleaning-service employees was more challenging than supervising workers with more gratifying jobs. I am not sure that was accurate, judging from events still to come; however, supervising the group was challenging. To be an effective leader, one must develop a trust factor. I supervised about eight workers and found that only a few were secure enough with themselves that they did not concern themselves with me or my instructions. They knew what they were required to do and went about their daily business with little or no supervision; however, they remained just a little bit suspicious of me. As an example, I had an early encounter with one of the senior employees. I approached him while he was cleaning in his area and asked him, "How long have you been here?" He became defensive and immediately began to tell me that he had not been in the area longer than he should have. I stopped him in midsentence and informed him that I was asking how long he had been with the Postal Service. He soon realized I was not a micromanager. After my clarification, he began to loosen up and talked freely with me, and I started building trust among the group.

As this was the mid 1970s, not far removed from the Jim Crow area, one White employee made a racially charged remark to me. The employee appeared to be a bit slow but did not have a problem stating what he felt. On a night when everyone was standing around the time clock waiting to clock in, this White cleaner told me that he was not going to be supervised by a "colored" man. I was not offended because I truly believed he was not all there. Therefore, I just dismissed what he said. I told him that even though he did not like being supervised by a colored man, he had to be supervised by someone, so it may as well be me. He just laughed and went on his way. To confirm my suspicions about his mental stability, I had a conversation with him one night in which he mentioned killing himself because of family problems. I talked to him for a while and convinced him that there had to be other options. He did seem to have a very low IQ and was easily manipulated or convinced. It appeared my conversation with him was successful, however.

Some time after the "colored man" comment, I learned that my previous station manager had heard about the incident and that he was proud of how I had handled it. He was especially proud because on his original belief that I harbored racist attitudes toward White people. I am sure he felt proud that he had recommended me for the position and that I had not gone off when I was called a colored man, which was no longer an acceptable term in the Black community. I often wondered how my former manager became aware of the incident and if the whole thing were a setup to see how I would handle it.

I also ran into some subtle discrimination while supervising the janitors. One evening, I was talking to one of the female clerks who was working on the workroom floor. I made a point to not stop her from working, but that was not good enough. One of the floor supervisors walked up to me, in front of the young lady, and told me to not interfere with his clerks while they were working. It ticked me off, but he was a higher-level supervisor and I complied. However, the more I though about it, the more I wanted to get the situation straightened out. I spoke to one of the other White supervisors with whom I had carried mail and asked him what the guy's problem was. Without hesitation, he told me the guy was prejudiced. Later, I told the supervisor that I did not like how he had approached me, that I was also a supervisor, and that I knew not to interfere with employees while working. Believe it or not, he apologized to me, and I did not have any further problems with him.

On another occasion, I was in the swing room where several supervisors were playing dominoes. I was there to talk with one of the Black supervisors with whom I had developed a friendship, but one of the White supervisors made a wisecrack, telling me that I needed to go back to the workroom floor and clean up the trash. Never at a loss of words, I responded that I would wait a while until all the trash was on the floor. He shut up.

Supervisory duties also had many unpleasant moments, as well. I had to talk to one of the employees about proper hygiene. This cleaner would report to work and light up the whole area. I put off talking to him as long as I could, but enough was enough. When I confronted him, he told me he had a medical problem.

I replied that this explanation did not suffice because he did not smell like that all the time. He reported to work in a better condition, which was good for all of us who had to breathe in his presence.

My tenure as building service supervisor included some interesting times. Part of my duties included walking the entire complex to make sure everything was in order. The main post office was located in downtown Fort Worth, and many homeless people came into the post office to get out of the elements and for other reasons. One night while making my rounds, I was walking through the stairwell and approaching the third floor of the building when I encountered a very foul odor. I looked down and realized that I had almost stepped in a very serious deposit left on the steps by one of the homeless individuals. That was one of the strongest odors I have ever encountered. Now, do you recall the cleaner who referred to me as a colored man? Well I had a job for him to perform. I instructed him to get the necessary cleaning equipment, proceed to the steps leading to the third floor, and clean up the mess. I specifically told him to use Pine-Sol to neutralize the smell. The best that I recall, the Pine-Sol was neutralized.

During a very cold night, some homeless people climbed inside a dumpster and built a fire to stay warm. Smoke began emitting from the dumpster, and someone called the fire department, thinking the dumpster had caught fire. When the firefighters began shooting water into the dumpster, two homeless men jumped out, one with a scorched nose. On another night, the postal guard (a position that no longer exists) was making his rounds and noticed water running out of the lobby telephone booth. He knew that did not make any sense because there was no water in that area. He went to the telephone booth, opened the door, and found a homeless man on his knees, urinating. He made the man take his coat off and mop up the urine.

One of my employees who was assigned as a cleaner seemed to be out of place in that position. He stopped by my office one night when I had my books out, studying for one my management classes, and he began talking management theories with me. I do not know if he was trying to impress me or not, but he seemed to be a little too knowledgeable about things you would not expect the average cleaner to know. He was also very articulate, and I began wondering why he was functioning in the capacity of a cleaner. One day he revealed to me that he had taken many management courses while in the Air Force. He had come to the Fort Worth office in the only position that was open at that time, and he was hoping to move into other areas. After talking with him on several occasions, I knew it was only a matter of time before he would move up. He eventually rose to one of the highest managerial positions in the Fort Worth post office. Everything was not always peaches and cream with him, however. I had to exercise my supervisory skills in response to his getting himself into an unpleasant position. I overheard him really putting down a couple of cleaners one night and telling them he was going places while they would remain cleaners because they were not capable of doing anything different. After hearing that, I had to chastise him for putting the other employees down. I told him that even though some may have reached their potential, it was not very commendable of him to gloat about his abilities and at the same time put others down because of their shortcomings.

While working in Maintenance, my wife and I went to the annual Christmas party that was put on by the Postal Credit Union. We made our way to a table to sit, and just as we were getting settled, the unexpected happened. A young White woman who also worked in the Maintenance office saw me coming in, ran over to me, and asked me to dance. Now, even though things were changing in race relations—this was now 1975—or 1976—I did not believe they had changed that much. However, to not embarrass the young lady, I agreed, and we proceeded to the dance floor. I knew all eyes were on me, or so I thought. We danced, and I knew I had to do something that would at least satisfy those who were watching. Some likely believed that I was one of those Black guys who worked around White women, could not help myself, and had to get me one. So, thinking while dancing, I decided that as soon as we finished dancing, I would take the young lady over and introduce her to my wife. Anyone who thought something was going on between the two of us had to have known I was not so good that I could introduce my "plaything" to my wife. I believe that ended any speculations.

After working in Maintenance for approximately two years, I began to get a little antsy and wanted to move up. I visited the manager of Distribution about an opportunity to work in the Mail Processing section. His name was Willie Hathman, and he happened to be the highest-ranking Black manager in the history of the Fort Worth post office. He said that there were not any openings but that he would keep me in mind.

I also went to the Personnel Office and met the manager of Employee Relations, who had the responsibility of posting all positions, including supervisory and managerial positions.

I inquired about what I needed to do to become a regular supervisor, explaining that I had completed over three years in college and planned to graduate in about a year. He seemed to take a liking to me and introduced me to his boss, the manager of Employee and Labor Relations. The manager also seemed to see something in me that he liked and asked me if I would be interested in a detail in labor relations. I did not even know what that was at that time, but I immediately said yes. He gave me a stack of books to read and told me that, once I digested the information, I should get back with him for a possible detail. I explained to him that I was attending summer school and did not have a lot of time to study the material, but as soon as summer school was over, I would read the books and get back with him. He told me that was fine.

This was a time in the Postal Service when there was an active movement to diversify certain functional areas. The diversity in the personnel office included two Hispanics, a female secretary, and a male equal employment opportunity counselor. There were no Black employees in the personnel office.

In fact, in 1975 and 1976, there was one Black station manager and two Black supervisors who worked with the public in Customer Services, Station and Branches. Approximately five supervisors worked on tour 1 in mail processing, and there were one Black tour superintendent and a Black manager of Distribution in the Mail Processing Department.

The labor relation detail was a very good position, and the labor relations department was an elite, well-respected part of the post office. However, all was not as it appeared. After completing my summer college courses, I studied the material the manager had provided me. I went to his office to return it, and I advised him that I had completed the task and was still interested in the offer. The manager asked me where I had been, saying that he had expected me back much sooner. I reminded him of what I had told him and said that I had just completed my summer courses. He apologized to me and told me they had selected someone else for the detail. At the time, I thought I had made a huge mistake and felt terrible about it. I asked the manager if I could just hang around in the office to gain as much information as I could. He told me I could. I soon realized that I was not going to get the detail because the person in charge of labor relations made the selection and filled the detail—not the manager—and I was not in the running. As I hung around the personnel office, I soon realized why.

One day the labor relations representative put on a little show on my behalf. I was standing in his door as he talked to the person he had selected to train as a labor relations assistant. He began talking about managers who were close to retirement age and wondered out loud who would or could replace them. The manager of Mail Processing was approaching retirement age, and the Labor Relations representative stated, in my presence, that there was no one qualified to take the manager's place when he retired. I truly believe the comment was made because I was there, and I also I thought his statement was strange, mainly because the person who was next in line in mail processing was the well-respected Black manager of Distribution, Willie Hathman. I believe the labor representative's whole intent was to put the Black manager down in my presence by indicating that he was not capable or qualified to replace the White manager, especially knowing that all the talk around the post office indicated that the Black manager was the heir apparent.

I took his comments personally, which I believe was his intent; not only was the Black manager not good enough to succeed the White manager of Mail Processing, in his estimation, I was not good enough to work for him as a Labor Relations assistant. To this day, I believe that was the message he was trying to convey to me. His comments later came back to play a role in a very important selection.

I went back to my position in Maintenance with the realization that I had a difficult task before me in my attempt to move up in the Postal Service. However, strange things by even stranger people began to take place. The same manager who did not want me in the labor assistant detail approached me and informed me that the EEO counselor position was being advertised for promotion. I am not sure if he came to me of his on volition or if the personnel manager encouraged him to tell me. Either way, I was happy about the notice, but I did suspect I was being told because of the way the other job situation had played out. I applied for the position but did not have a clue as to what the position required.

I was scheduled for an interview. I thought and hoped that my educational background and being close to having my degree would benefit me and put me in good shape to get the promotion. When I reported for the interview, I was pleasantly surprised that the person chairing the interview board was the manager of Employee Relations, the same person who had introduced me to the office manager earlier. Seeing him caused me to relax a little, and the interviewing process went well. I did not know some things about EEO that I should have known, but I was able to answer most of the management-type questions, which allowed me to place in the top three. I did not realize it at the time, but that was all I needed to do—place in the top three and the position was mine. I believe the decision to award me the job was at least partially based on my being denied the labor relations assistant position. In fact, that detail was made a permanent position around the same time I received the promotion to the EEO counselor position. One thing that must be said is that, while the EEO job was a good promotion for me, it was not at the same level and did not have the same prestige as the labor relations position. Read into that what you like.

# Chapter 10

## Fourth Stage of Going Postal

### Human Resources

I was very proud of what I had accomplished and felt I was on my way after receiving the promotion to EEO counselor. However, I still had concerns about who I was and what I could accomplish in life. I had accomplished a lot so far, but I was still not sure of myself. I reflected on my high school experiences, where I rose to be the commander of the NDCC. I reflected on work experiences, where my first job at a particular company was washing cars and I was later promoted to assistant manager of the get-ready department. I reflected on being drafted and then graduating from Special Warfare School and becoming a sergeant in the Special Forces. However, I still lacked confidence in my abilities for some reason.

I believe my lack of confidence stemmed from my childhood. I was the youngest of four and grew up being dominated by my older brothers, especially the one closest to me in age. He had it all, and I was just there. I started school when I was five and soon realized I was behind the other kids in my class. I was not very successful in my early school years. I struggled for many years trying to catch up to the other kids, and some of the smarter kids called me dumb. I am not sure I believed I was dumb, but I did have internal questions about my abilities.

In relation to the promotion, I spoke with a friend of mine about my anxiety and said I hoped I would be able to perform the duties of the EEO counselor's position. This friend, who was a college-educated chemist, assured me I could do the job. He saw more in me than I saw in myself at the time, and his words helped my fears subside, to a degree. However, I was still in the process of being defined, and I had adjustments to make.

When I reported to the personnel department, it seemed that most of the employees there were receptive and did not have a problem with a Black person working among them. One attractive woman in the office befriended me, and she seemed to not have any hang-ups about the first Black male employee in the Fort Worth personnel office.

To set the tone in the office, especially regarding women, the manager called me to his office one morning a day or two after I started to lay down a few of his rules. The main one was designed to warn me about fraternizing with the women in the office. He told me, "Do not dip your pen in the company's ink." I got the message, and I followed those instructions. One other thing he told me was to not tell him what I thought he wanted to hear but what I thought. I truly appreciated that message.

The manager was a workaholic; he was the first in the office in the morning and the last one there at night. I had always heard that if you wanted to impress your boss, beat him to work and do not leave until after he does. I tried that for a few weeks, but I decided I was not going to let that notion kill me. I kept decent hours, but I had a home life and young boys to engage with.

After I began working in the office, I was asked all kind of questions about Black people, as if I were the spokesperson. I was asked why young Black men and women who came to the personnel office were so loud. Well, as the Black spokesperson, I figured I had an answer. I responded that, for many years, young Blacks could not speak out about anything, and now that things were changing, they were enjoying their new freedom of expression, no matter how loud.

Shortly after receiving the promotion to EEO counselor, I headed to our Southern Regional Office to participate in classroom training. I was accompanied on the trip by the Hispanic EEO counselor who worked in the office with me. He was not only an EEO counselor, but the regional office used him on many Southern Region projects. I later realized that he was important in the region.

At the training, I met a group of high-level Black managers, which I was not accustomed to seeing, especially since all the supervisors and managers I knew in Fort Worth were not at their levels. The manager of Employee Relations for the entire Southern Region was a Black man named Kenneth Whalen. That name is significant, and I will discuss him later. He came before the group of trainees and gave us a pep talk. I was thoroughly impressed with his oratorical skills, and I hung on his every word.

Next, the manager of the EEO branch spoke to our group. She was an attractive, well-developed Black woman, and she was also most impressive. A couple other managers were there but played a lesser role in the training process even though they were important in the EEO department.

The training sessions were informative, and I learned a lot about the process. One of the first questions posed to the group was whether we were prejudiced. The first thing that crossed my mind was that I had been asked that same question when I interviewed for my first promotional opportunity, and I remembered how I responded then. I volunteered to answer the question. I said that I was indeed prejudiced but clarified that I was not racially prejudiced. That was the answer the group was looking for, and the EEO counselor and representative from Fort Worth, who was one of the facilitators, complimented me on it.

While there in Memphis, one of the EEO managers invited a select group of us out to his residence for food, drinks, and fun. I was happy to attend. Earlier, during breaks in the training, some of us sat around telling our best jokes, and I noticed that this manager did not seem to enjoy my joke and seemed very dismissive. But since he had asked me to attend his gathering, I thought that maybe he had liked my joke after all. In fact, I realized he loved good jokes and had plenty himself. We became good friends, and his name will come up later.

I worked as an EEO counselor for approximately nine months, and during that period, I graduated from Texas Wesleyan College with a degree in business administration. This was probably the second-most significant event in my educational life, next to graduating from Special Warfare School at Fort Bragg. I was most proud of the fact that I had completed my college studies in five years while working full time. I had started college in January 1973 and graduated in December

1978. I took classes every summer except for one, when a class I needed was not available. I must give credit to my wife for supporting me, not making many demands of me, and keeping the kids away from me while I studied.

While working in Human Resources, I was able to go all over the main post office and visit with many managers. During a push by some of the young Black employees to break into supervision, I visited some of the directors, especially the director of city delivery, or customer services, as it is now called, and learned that there was a long way to go to get Blacks promoted. At the same time I was inquiring and making an effort to improve things, two Black employees working in Station and Branches were both initially promoted into Mail Processing Operations, which did not face the public, but both had relevant experience, one as a carrier and one as a clerk. With one being male and the other female, it appeared that the director had concluded that he had met his diversity obligation. I figured this when I went to see him about the concerns of the others, and he informed me that he did not know another Black person who was qualified. Now what makes that statement important is that, at the time, postal managers did not consider the educational backgrounds of those they deemed qualified or ready for promotion. The decision was loosely based on a carrier or clerk passing the supervisor exam and then being recommended by the employee's manager. If a Black employee passed the examination but did not have a great working relationship with the station manager, he or she did not get promoted. During the period from 1977 to 1980, many Black postal employees were taking college courses under the GI Bill and were looking for opportunities. Education was a nonfactor for many upper-management personnel, mainly because there were few degreed people in upper management at that time.

I was taken aback by the manager's comment about a lack of qualified Black employees because he was implying that I was not qualified even though I had recently graduated from college and was a former letter carrier. According to his comment, education did not mean anything. All previous promotions had been given to people without any experience other than being a clerk or carrier, who passed the supervisor examination, and who were not necessarily degreed.

Eventually, some of the same individuals who had initially been denied opportunities during that period rose to managerial positions in Station and Branches. I will elaborate on that situation later.

While working as an EEO counselor, I realized I was very gullible. I believed people were basically honest and that, when they told me something, they were being truthful. I did not believe people would lie about things such as being discriminated against. One thing I quickly learned was that White employees complained of discrimination as much as, if not more than, minority employees. I was not aware of that prior to working in EEO. I also became aware that people would claim discrimination about almost anything, no matter how frivolous. When I was informed of a discrimination claim, I would go to the workroom floor. Most of the supervisors I encountered saw me as the enemy and as the voice of the employee complaining of discrimination. I got nowhere when trying to determine whether an employee truly was a victim of discrimination. If the record review did not support disparate treatment, there was nothing else I could do, and for the entire period that I was an EEO counselor, I was not able to establish that any one employee was a victim of discrimination.

I was sent on a few projects while working as an EEO counselor. The EEO specialist, who worked out of the Dallas office, sent me to Temple, Texas, to conduct EEO counseling. This was my first trip outside Fort Worth to perform any duties. I enjoyed the experience, even though I was still learning the job duties.

The manager of employee and labor relations asked me later to go to Wichita Falls, Texas, to recruit minorities for clerk and carrier positions. He felt the action was needed based on that office's hiring practices. No minorities were employees in the Wichita Falls office other than those working as custodians. In preparation, I had to spend time with the manager of Employee Development while he conducted training classes for prospective applicants on taking the postal examination.

My task in Wichita Falls was to meet with the local community leaders, make them aware of the plan, and get them to advertise the training that would take place. I met with the local leaders in the Black and Hispanic communities and set up the training. My efforts were appreciated by the local participants, and the carrier and clerk positions at Wichita Fall were integrated a year or so later. I felt good about that accomplishment.

I did have an incident while driving home from Wichita Falls, however. This little town called Bowie was on the way and had a reputation for ticketing Blacks who drove through their community. I had stopped to get a cup of coffee and placed the coffee in the cupholder. The cup got stuck in the cupholder as I was leaving the drive-thru restaurant, and I was fumbling with the cup, trying not to spill the coffee. My foot was on the gas pedal, and I did not realize that I was exceeding the speed limit. Before I knew it, I saw flashing lights, and a highway patrolman behind me pulled me over for speeding. I did not say a word and just took the ticket.

I did not know much about how small-town post offices and their postmasters worked, but I was under the illusion that the postmaster, as a political figure in those days, had influence in the town and could get things done. I mentioned to the manager of Employee and Labor Relations that I had gotten a ticket leaving Bowie and asked him to contact the local postmaster to see if he could take care of it. The manager told me he was not sure he could help but that he would talk to our postmaster, who was the manager of all the smaller post offices in our Management Sectional Center. A few days later, my manager told me that the postmaster had asked him what I was doing in Wichita Falls on a Saturday. My manager told him that I had conducted a training class that day, but the postmaster told my manager that the Bowie postmaster could not help. The postmaster offered to pay me overtime for working on a Saturday, though, which more than covered the ticket expense. I learned a few valuable lessons—that small-town postmasters did not have any power; if I had to work on Saturday as an exempt employee, there was a way to get paid; and I needed to be more careful driving through small-town Texas.

While serving as the local EEO counselor, I had the opportunity to meet several individuals who came to Fort Worth to investigate EEO discrimination complaints. I developed a great relationship with a few that lasted for the rest of my postal career. When the investigators came to town, I would normally take them home with me and on occasion provide them evening meals. Later in my postal career, I would be reunited with them once again.

Approximately nine months later, a new position was advertised for promotion. Employees who sustained injuries were being managed through the Safety Office, and all the related paperwork was completed and forwarded to the Department of Labor, where it was processed through the Postal Service's Safety Office. Due to a growing number of claims being filed, the decision was made to separate that work from safety and establish the Office of Injury Compensation. The position was advertised as an EAS-16, and as an EEO counselor, I was in a hybrid ACS-15 position. I do not recall what the letters stood for, but I was in a category that did not apply to many others, and it was in a low pay grade. I went to the personnel manager and informed him that I wanted the new position because the EEO counselor's position was thought of as a minority position, and I did not want to be in a minority position. He looked at me rather strangely, told me to apply, and said he would consider me.

# Chapter 11

## Fifth Stage of Going Postal

### Human Resources Part 2

I applied for the newly established Injury Compensation supervisor position, and my main competition came from a Postal Service nurse. I was selected for the position and soon on my way.

It must be noted that after being promoted to Injury Compensation Supervisor, another significant person came into my life. I was asked to serve on the selection committee for my replacement as an EEO Counselor. During the interview process, I met an applicant from Dallas, TX, James Brown, who was impressive and was a Union Steward in the Dallas Post Office. James, better known as J.D., was selected for the position, and became only the second Black person to work in the Fort Worth personnel office. Over time, we became very close friends, and especially after I met his wife and he met mine. We were frequent visitors in each other's home and the friendship flourished for many years.

As time rocked on, I gained more and more confidence in my abilities, and I quickly caught on to the duties of the position.

The personnel manager was a very shrewd individual, and he promoted his personal secretary, who was a very efficient person, to work with me as my assistant. She would manage the incoming and outgoing files related to injury claims. I believe he promoted her for two reasons: so she could ensure that I did not fail, and because he was very fond of her and her work ethics. Whatever the reason, it became immaterial, and we developed a very good working relationship. She was a very sharp person, she kept me focused, and I grew in the position.

We often engaged in conversation during idle times, and I was amaze at what she did not know about the races, more specifically about Black people. I had not had many conversations with a woman of a different race up to that point, and I found her conversation and lack of Black and White history interesting. For example, she did not know why some people within the Black race were different colors. She was not aware that breeding during slavery had created a subrace of people, said to be of mixed race. I told her that the slave owners, by and large, had their way with the Black female slaves, under threat of killing their mates, which produced some Blacks who looked white, almost white, very light, light brown, and in some cases dark with straight or very curly or wavy hair. We had a saying in the Black community when describing our people as very light or high yellow, "brother" or "sister." We would also say a brother or sister was light, bright, and damn near white. In relation to how Blacks were treated in the larger society, we in the Black community had a saying: if you are white, you are all right; if you are brown, stick around; if you are black, get back.

After educating my assistant on why Blacks were of different colors, I mentioned my wife, whom she had met, and explained that my wife's great-grandfather was White, and that was why she was lighter in color. My assistant was enlightened, and I could not believe she had not known.

One of the things my manager told me upon my promotion to Injury Compensation supervisor was that I needed to look at every injury claim filed by employees as fraudulent. He explained that if I scrutinized every case as if it involved fraud, I would not miss a case where fraud actually existed. I went about my work very diligently.

In reviewing case files, I came across several suspicious claims. One case I reviewed involved an employee who was unable to work and had been relegated to limited work, doing very little. In reading the case file, I saw that the employee's doctor had written a letter to the Department of Labor stating that his patient should not be skiing. I thought that was strange because the employee was not able to perform any work duties but evidently was skiing, which her physician did not condone.

After reviewing records and determining that employees were doing other things outside the work environment that all but supported the idea that they were able to perform limited or light-duty work at the post office but refused to return to work based on a doctor's very subjective statements, I mailed out letters. These employees were informed of the newly discovered evidence and instructed to report for duty. If they were not able to report, separation letters would be issued based on their being in a leave-without-pay status for over a year or so—I do not recall the specifics. In several instances, employees returned to work rather than risk separation.

There was a problem, however. Some employees who were under suspicion of fraud should not have been. For example, I learned of an employee with a back condition, but his supervisor suspected he was not truly injured. One day the employee came to my office, and I saw for the first time someone with a back injury. What I saw was something that a person could not fake. This man's body was twisted, and his upper body was not in alignment with his lower body. I was convinced that he was truly an injured employee, and that changed my perspective. I started looking at cases with a more compassionate eye.

However, my investigative skills were about to be tested. I met with one employee with whom the Postal Service was having all kinds of problems. She continuously claimed she could perform little or no work. When we met, I closed the office door for privacy when I spoke with her. I did not have a clue about who or what I was dealing with. My assistant told me that I had to be very careful with female employees and that I should never close the door when meeting with them. I understood what she was saying, and that never happened again. Fortunately, nothing happened, but the story was just beginning.

In reviewing the employee's injury file, I could not figure out how she had sustained the supposed injury from her description of how it happened. The woman's wrist was almost destroyed, according to her, and I thought she had caught her arm in the machinery on the workroom floor. In reviewing her file carefully, all I saw was that she was lifting a tray of mail that weighed fifteen pounds or less and injured her wrist. I personally could not see how she could sustain the reported damage to her wrist by lifting around fifteen pounds.

I was not satisfied with the information that suggested she had a permanent condition, where she basically could not use her right hand because of the wrist injury. In looking at her employment application as part of my background investigation, I noticed something that raised all kind of red flags.

Prior to continuing, I would like to give a little background information on my investigation. A few years prior to this, there was a highly publicized murder case in Fort Worth where a wealthy man was on trial for shooting his wife and killing his wife's boyfriend. In reading all the information about that case that I could, the name of a karate studio owner surfaced in the murder case and stuck with me.

Back to my investigating the employee's injury and reviewing her application for postal employment. This employee used the karate studio owner as her personal reference. It did not take a genius to figure out how her wrist had been so severely injured, and working at the Postal Service was not the reason. The only problem with my discovery was that I could not prove the connection. However, the story continues, and later in this book, we will revisit this most interesting employee.

In working as the Injury Compensation supervisor, I noticed something that seemed to be a pattern. I ran across a few names that I had previously noticed while working as an EEO counselor.

I worked in the Injury Compensation office for nine months, had really learned the job, and believed I was doing everything my boss had hoped I would accomplish. However, a situation was about to come full circle.

The labor relations representative had received a promotion, and the office brought in a new labor representative. The person promoted to the position I was initially asked to be detailed to was also promoted to the now-vacant manager of Employee Relations position, which left a vacancy in Labor Relations. The position was an EAS-16, the same level of my current position, and I now had an opportunity to work in Labor Relations if I wanted to.

After thinking about the situation and weighing my options, I went to the manager and told him that I wanted to make a lateral move into the newly vacant Labor Relations position. He stated he would think about it and later agreed to allow me the lateral transfer to the EAS-16 labor relations assistant position.

# Chapter 12

## Sixth Stage of Going Postal

### Human Resources Part 3

At the time, I believed that I was on my way. With my promotion to supervisor, I had become a member of the management team, a member of the highly respected Labor Relations staff, or so I thought. The position was everything I thought it would be, and even though it took me a while to get my feet under me, I loved every minute of my new position.

My duties consisted of writing minor discipline reports and handling grievances involving the three major unions: the American Postal Workers Union (APWU), the largest union at the time, which represented all Clerk Craft, Special Delivery Craft, Motor Vehicle Craft, and Maintenance Craft employees; the National Association of Letter Carriers (NALC); and the National Postal Mail Handler Union (NPMHU). On occasion, I was also assigned grievances filed by the National Rural Letter Carrier Association (NRLCA).

Some of the union stewards smelled fresh meat, and in their initial meetings with me, they attempted to intimidate me by playing the role of the big bad union representative. I told each representative who was trying to use psychology against me that, if they were trying to intimidate me, I was too dumb to understand the psychology of it. I told them a story about my boxing hero, Muhammad Ali, and the time he fought Joe Frazier. Ali tried to use psychology on Frazier in an attempt to confuse him, but it did not work. Frazier admitted that he did not understand what Ali was trying to do; all he knew to do was attack Ali. In that first fight, Frazier did not fall into Ali's little trap, and he whipped Ali. Ever since, there has been a standing joke that Joe Frazier was too dumb to understand any psychological tricks and whipped Ali's butt.

I told each union representative that if he had a legitimate grievance, I would do what I could to work with him to get it resolved, but I would not fall for games or any attempt to intimidate me.

As I was being broken in and trying to learn as much as I could in my new position, I discovered that I was scheduled to attend a three-week labor relations training course in Washington, DC. Under normal circumstances, I would not have been scheduled for the class until working several months in the position, but my predecessor had scheduled it but not attended, so I took the slot that was originally his.

Off to Washington I went on my first trip for training purposes. I was a little apprehensive about the trip and hoped I knew enough about labor relations at the time to not make a fool of myself. Once I got to DC, I had a pleasant surprise. One person in the class was from Beaumont, Texas, and I had met him when I was in the EEO position. He and I hit it off right away, and we hung out while in DC. I also made acquaintances with several trainees from all over the United States.

Once trained, I felt like I was able to take on more responsibilities as a labor relations representative. However, there were hurdles to overcome. The manager of Employee and Labor Relations had his own procedures for his labor staff. He met with my supervisor, the labor relations representative, and me and told us that our job was to support Operations management in all our grievance hearings; and if we could not resolve the issue with Operation's approval, we were to deny the grievance and let it go to step three of the grievance procedure. According to the contract with the unions, we were the postmaster's step-two designees, and we were to process all grievances with full authority to settle, modify, or deny them. However, the manager took that authority from us. I was in a very frustrating position because Operations managers violated the contract at will, knowing they would not be overruled, at least at the local level.

Not long after being promoted, I was introduced to a demanding part of my new job that was at times the most gratifying and at other times the most disappointing. That was the arbitration process, which came about after a grievance processed through the steps of the procedure without a resolution being reached. The union would then appeal the case, and it would go into arbitration.

Working on a case to present before an arbitrator was scary and challenging. The process called for knowing all the facts of the case, preparing the witnesses to testify about the steps they took in the process, and presenting witnesses and documentation to the arbitrator to assure him or her that proper procedures were followed and that the articles of the union contract were not violated.

The first case I was assigned to present before an arbitrator involved a seven-day suspension issued to a female employee for failing to report for work on a snow or ice day. The issuing supervisor testified that he charged the female with being absent without official leave (AWOL) and issued her the suspension because she failed to report for duty and failed to notify anyone that she could not report. The supervisor stated that, in coming to his determination to discipline the employee, he had stepped outside the main office and saw that traffic was moving well and that ice did not seem to be a problem on the streets.

While the employee was on the stand as a witness for herself, I asked her if she had tried to report for duty, and she answered that she had. I asked her how far she had gotten in her attempt, and she answered that she had driven to the back dock but was listening to the weather report and decided to drive back home when she heard that more snow and ice would fall that night.

I felt that her admission that she had made it to work but decided to leave was all that was needed for me to prevail in my first arbitration case. My boss even told me later that I had done a good job and that had not presented myself like it was my first case. I was looking for a win. But in the arbitration decision, the union prevailed. The arbitrator, in his decision, taught me a valuable lesson that I remembered for future discipline. He ruled against the post office because the supervisor had failed to talk to the employee prior to charging her with being AWOL. The supervisor testified that, after he went outside to check the streets, he went back in and charged her as AWOL on the same day. According to the just-cause principles, as required by Article

16 of the agreement, the supervisor was required to give the employee an opportunity to explain why she had not reported and then, based on her explanation, make a decision about whether to approve or deny her leave. Lesson learned.

Something else happened in the first arbitration case that caused me to reevaluate remaining in that position. After coming out of the arbitration hearing, I developed what I assume was a migraine headache. I had never had a migraine or headaches of any severity. I informed my boss that I was ill and needed to go home. After arriving at home, I took aspirin, had a strong drink, and went to bed. I had a conversation with my wife, and she told me that if the affected me so negatively, I should find something else to do. I have quit only one thing in my life and always regretted it, and I was not about to quit my Labor Relations job. So I needed to figure out what had caused the headache and try to figure out what I needed to do to fix the problem. I thought about how I would get a minor headache when I did not eat by noon. Especially during that time, I was not eating breakfast on workdays. In recalling that, I decided to make a point of eating breakfast, especially on arbitration hearing days. I also realized that I had to learn to relax while in arbitration, even though there was very little room to do so as I had to stay on top of every word said. But I did learn to relax a little, and I never had another headache like that.

I had developed a good working relationship with two important union officials. The first was the area vice president with the Mail Handler Union. He was of Hispanic heritage and joy to work with. He knew I was learning my job, and he was always open and respectful toward me. I believe he was aware that I had restraints on what I could and could not do in relation to solving grievances. I also developed a good working relationship with the Tour 1 and Tour 3 Union Representatives for the APWU. The Tour 3 steward was an Italian New Yorker, and the Tour 1 steward was a Black guy who had grown up in the Lake Como community of Fort Worth.

The NALC president dealt only with my boss, the Labor Relations representative, and one day I overheard a conversation they were having. The president called one of the acting Black supervisors a baboon. That did not sit well with me. I stopped what I was doing, and stepped into the hallway to the room, and let him know I had heard his comment. He attempted to assure me it was not a racist comment. I did not believe him, but I went on about my business and let it slide. We never did develop a close working relationship, but over time we had opportunities to work through problems.

Eventually, things started changing. The manager of Employee and Labor Relations grew fond of me, and we developed a good working relationship. It was still difficult to do the job I felt I was hired for because Labor Relations did not have autonomy in making needed decisions.

The manager seemed to favor me over my supervisor and offered me a detail in our Southern Regional Office as a labor relations specialist. It was still early in my learning curve in Labor Relations, so I turned down the offer, not realizing the benefits that could come from such a detail.

As time passed, I gained more and more experience in handling grievances and in arbitrating cases. I also presented cases before administrative judges with the EEOC and the Merit System Protection Board (MSPB).

My arbitration win ratio was not that good initially, and I always surmised that my boss was cherry-picking cases. My win ratio hovered somewhere around 50 percent, and my boss's was always somewhere around 70 to 75percent. However, one way that we started improving was that I took on the task of writing all disciplinary letters. Discipline cases were easier to win when all the correct steps were taken. Our office also handled a few contract cases, and we could handle those that were not precedent-setting cases. The Labor Relations specialist from the Southern Regional Office handled those. My boss handled most of the nonprecedent contract cases that were appealed to arbitration and most of the well-prepared discipline cases.

During this time, we made a trip to Houston for a labor relations training session, and the manager of Employee and Labor Relations made the trip with us. The session included Labor Relations personnel from Louisiana and Texas. I had an opportunity to again see the labor representative from Beaumont whom I had first met when he was an EEO investigator.

After our class was over, everyone was trying to determine where they wanted to go to let off a little steam. I do not recall how the decision was made, but we ended up at a strip joint on the outskirts of Houston. Other than when I was approximately nineteen or twenty and living in Compton, I had not been in a strip joint. All the young men in Southern California frequented Tijuana, Mexico, and that was where I saw my first striptease show.

Once we were seated inside, I was looking at one woman who, from a distance, appeared to be Black, but she had very fair skin so I was not sure. Shortly after she left the stage, she appeared in front of me in a red dress and began dancing. Soon, she took off her dress and threw it in my direction. I ducked, and the dress wrapped around the head of my friend from Beaumont. I soon realized this was the same woman I had been looking at to determine her ethnicity, and yes, she was Black. She approached me and whispered in my ear, "All night long for a hundred dollars." I politely replied, "No, thanks." I looked at my watch and saw that it was close to three in the morning. I wondered, *What was she going to do to me before the sun came up that would be worth a hundred dollars.* Then, to my surprise, she propositioned each of the men in our group, and they quickly turned her down. However, when she got to the manager of Employee and Labor Relations, he began to negotiate with her, and she remained there for a while. I thought he was going to make the deal, but evidently, he was not able to get the price he wanted. And then she came back to me with two big bouncers standing behind her. She said in a loud voice, "Which one of you m-----f-----s is going to pay for my dance?" I quickly replied, "Lady, I did not ask you come over here." I told the group that I thought it was time for us to get out of there before trouble started. We quickly left.

In my supervisory position, I had developed a great working relationship with the manager. I had developed confidence in what I was doing and was looking for greener pastures. I knew the labor representative was looking to get promoted, and I was positioning myself for his position. But there was a problem: I had developed a relationship with the attractive woman in the office I previously mentioned. Even though we were just friends, we spent time in each other's company and a woman in another office in the building started rumors that we were an item. This woman had a Black assistant to whom she mentioned her suspicions of this alleged relationship. The Black assistant was a friend of mine, and she came to ask me if I had heard the latest rumors. I said no. She informed me that it was all over the post office that the attractive woman and I were in a relationship. The information shocked me, and the first thing I thought about was the advice the office manager had given me about office relationships. Based on those concerns, I walked into the manager's office and asked him if he had heard any rumors about me. He said he had not. I informed him that rumors about me and the woman were floating around the office. I assured him that nothing was going on and they were just rumors. I said that I was ambitious and too concerned about my career to jeopardize it by having an affair with one of the women in the office. He told me to not worry about the rumors and said everything was okay. As I turned to walk out of his office, he asked, "How was it?" I turned around with a smile on my face and assured him again they were just rumors. He seemed disappointed with my answer and just smiled as I left.

One other problem developed as I tried to establish some credibility in Labor Relations. For the record, Willie Hathman was promoted to manager of Mail Processing, the position the original Labor Representative did not think he was qualified to fill. That left a vacancy for the manager of Distribution Operations position, which was filled by the former manager of Employee Relations, with whom I thought I had a good working relationship. After receiving a request for a seven-day suspension from one of his supervisors, I went to his office to discuss how to improve the discipline request. The employee involved in the incident had a late-reporting problem, and for his most recent late-reporting absence, he was granted approved leave. I explained to the manager that, since the employee had a problem getting to work on time, the disciplinary action would have been stronger if the supervisor had disapproved the last leave request after the employee reported late and then charged the employee as being AWOL. He disagreed with my recommendation, and after further discussion, I guess he tired of me and told me that I did not run Mail Processing. I was not going to be outdone. I told him that he was absolutely correct, but I reminded him that I had authority to make decisions on grievances that were appealed to step 2two of the grievance procedure. That comment did not sit well with him.

As time passed, I built relationships with many of the floor supervisors, particularly one with whom I had a run in when I was the Maintenance supervisor. He was the one who had confronted me about talking with one of his clerk employees. But when he needed to talk to someone in Labor Relations, he came by to see me.

As I said earlier, Willie Hathman was promoted to manager of Mail Processing, which was the second-most powerful manager position in the Fort Worth post office. He and I had developed a great working relationship over the years, and after I was promoted to Labor Relations assistant, he would come to visit me in my office. We would walk around the workroom floor in Mail Processing just discussing any- and everything. At the time, I was probably the only Black person at the main office with his own office and who could get up and move around the facility at will. On occasion, I would return the favor and visit his office. Willie was destined for greater things and moved around the country on various details that prepared him for a possible postmaster position.

The only postmaster I ever knew personally, Jack D. Watson, retired, and major jockeying for his position ensued. Willie was one of those in line for the promotion. He had just completed a detail as officer in charge at Galveston, Texas, a medium-size office not as large as Fort Worth. Willie applied for the Fort Worth position and was told, as he had been on several occasions after applying for postmaster positions, that he had done well and his time was coming. The position was awarded to someone else.

However, as fate would have it, the person who was awarded the postmaster's position at Fort Worth died unexpectedly, and Willie positioned himself where he could not be denied. Subsequently, he was promoted to postmaster of Fort Worth. Whereas many Northern cities had Black postmasters, Willie was one of very few Black managers in the South who was promoted to such a high-level position.

After Willie became postmaster, he visited each office complex to basically introduced himself. When he came to the Personnel Office, he stopped by each person's desk and inquired about how we were doing in our jobs. When he stopped by my office, I made the mistake of indirectly complaining about the work I was doing. For the record, I had the feeling that I was being dumped on by my immediate manager, the Labor Relations representative. I would go to his office and see that he was not doing much; in fact, he had a doodling pad on his clean desk, while my desk had a stack of grievances and other things to do. When Willie asked me about my work, I told him I was working ten-hour days and taking my work home on the weekend. I thought he would see what I was doing compared to my boss, but my presentation backfired. I soon learned that no one, including him, likes a complainer. He turned around to exit my office, then pivoted toward me and asked, "You are exempt, aren't you?" (An exempt employee earns a salary and is not paid overtime.) I felt like I was two feet tall, and I learned a valuable lesson.

After I was promoted to Labor Relations assistant, the person who had made a racist remark to me when I was a Maintenance supervisor was assigned to the supervisor of Injury Compensation position that I had vacated. After Willie was promoted to postmaster, this old nemesis came to my office and said, "You've got it made now." His comment ticked me off. I snapped back at him and asked if he had had it made when Jack Watson was postmaster, referring to the fact that Jack Watson was White since he thought I would benefit because Willie was Black. As a matter of fact, I made a point of not visiting the postmaster's office just to prevent anyone from thinking that I was trying to position myself for a future promotion. Willie even came to my office and asked why I was not dropping by as I had when he was the manager of Mail Processing.

Around the time of Willie's promotion, we had a vacancy in Human Resources. Willie was set to fill his second high-level position, that of manager of Personnel, which was changed to the manager of Human Resources. The selection process would be an interesting undertaking.

After the Personnel Manager retired, I had a new lease on life because I was able to address grievances based on merit instead of rubber-stamping them as the manager had required.

One of my early experiences with this newfound independence was a confrontation with the Tour 3 superintendent, the person I mentioned earlier who said I had it made. He sent one of his supervisors to Labor Relations with documentation to issue an employee a seven-day Suspension. The supervisor presented the documentation to me, and I asked him a few questions about the steps he had taken prior to making a request for discipline. I asked if he had talked to the employee about the charge, and he stated that he had not. So I informed him that he could not issue the discipline. This was unheard of and resulted in the Tour 3 superintendent's storming to my office to challenge me. When he walked in, he was fuming and as intimidating as ever, but once he completed his angry spiel and seemed to calm down, I had an opportunity to explain why the discipline request was inadequate. Once I did, he looked at me and asked, "We fucked up, didn't we?" I told him the steps he needed to take to issue effective discipline, and for a long period, he did not request any disciplinary actions without going through my office first.

Not all was necessarily well, however. The Southern Region Office sent out a team to survey the labor climate in Fort Worth, and the team interviewed the managers on all three tours. Labor Relations did not receive a good review, especially from the manager on Tour 1 and specifically about me as a Labor Relations assistant who handled Tour 1 grievances. He felt I did not support his tour's grievances and disciplines they were attempting to force through.

The team leader interviewed me to see what the problem was. I explained that, when I was investigating grievances, the supervisors and managers would not tell me the truth I needed in order to determine whether a violation existed. I further explained that as long as the Tour 1 management personnel did not tell me the truth, then, as the step-two designee, I would make the decision based on the information I had received in the grievance package. This was not a popular stand and differed from my immediate supervisor's, who would go along to get along.

I was catching flack not only from the supervisors and managers but also from the EEO investigators who had traveled to Fort Worth to investigate EEO complaints. At the time, in early 1980, all EEO investigators were working for the Southern Region Office but were domiciled all over the Southern Region states. Most of the investigators were hardnosed, civil-rights types who had come out of the old Alliance organization that protected the rights of mostly Black government workers, including postal workers, who in the early days could not join the White unions.

An investigator who was domiciled in Houston dropped by my office and put on a show in the presence of the labor representative, accusing everybody of discriminating against Black employees. That did not sit well with me, so I invited him to my office, closed the door, and lit into him. I was determined that he was not going to put me in that box. I was aware that several of the investigators thought that anyone working in Labor Relations was just a tool to further discriminate against Black employees. Some investigators even had a name for a Black person like me in the position I held. Well, that was not going to stand. Most of the investigators were originally representatives of the Alliance, and most were a few years older than me. To a large degree, they commanded respect from those with whom they dealt. I was not disrespectful, but there was no doubt what my role was when I finished with him. I made him aware that I saw my job as a gatekeeper. I made sure that the information coming to my desk was fair and that actions issued to Black employees were also being issued White employees. I told him that most discipline issued to employees was based on attendance deficiencies, and one way we were able to ensure equity in how discipline was being issued was by conducting attendance reviews of all employees. I am not sure if he accepted my presentation, but after that little talk, he did not play his little games with me again.

My record in arbitration was improving mainly because I was handling my own developed discipline cases. At the time, I did not handle contract cases since they were believed to be more complicated. They were handled either by the Labor Relations representative or labor representatives from the Southern Region Office.

During this period, I was also presenting discrimination cases before an EEOC administrative judge and removal cases before an administrative judge at the Merit System Protection Board, which mostly involved military veteran and management employees. The labor representative assigned all cases, and on one occasion, he assigned me a very difficult case that involved only circumstantial evidence. An employee was charged with destroying a piece of equipment that had been installed in postal jeeps to monitor the carrier's mileage and driving practices. The device would also indicate if an employee drove off his line of travel or drove more miles than authorized. The carrier in this case was accused of destroying the device so that he could not be tracked. On the day in question, when the carrier returned to the post office, the device in his jeep was not working, and all evidence suggested that he had sabotaged the equipment. In presenting the case before an arbitrator, I brought in a representative from the equipment manufacturer to testify about the equipment, the likelihood of its malfunctioning or being in the condition it was found in without human involvement, and the likelihood that it was destroyed by the letter carrier. After making our presentations, the union advocate suggested we go out to a vehicle and review the device firsthand to determine whether the manner in which the carrier loaded his vehicle may have contributed to the malfunction of the equipment. The union representative grabbed a tray of mail, threw it into the vehicle possibly as hard as he could, and slammed the tray against the equipment in an attempt to demonstrate, according to him, how a vehicle is loaded and how the equipment might have been damaged. He threw the mail tray so hard against the equipment that, if it were fragile, it would have broken. However, the cord flexed back into place, and his demonstration failed. I am not sure whether that demonstration sealed the win for me, but it surely did not hurt. The union representative looked very foolish in his demonstration.

I also handled a MSPB case during the same period that was very interesting. The person who appealed the case had a representative whom we called an outhouse lawyer. He had gained his reputation as a union steward who incidentally changed the steward structure in the Fort Worth post office. The guy's named was Lamar. and when he was a steward, the office used a formula to determine the number of stewards for each tour according to the number of employees on it. Lamar and a few other stewards were basically functioning as full-time stewards, and when they were not processing grievances for employees, the stewards were filing grievances for one another. Based on that activity, they did very little work, if any at all. The manager made a deal with the APWU union president, who agreed to have one full-time steward on each tour, thus eliminating the games the stewards were playing to avoid work. The change knocked Lamar out of the union office, and he then began representing employees in both EEO hearings and MSPB hearings.

The MSPB case I mentioned involved an injured employee. Lamar thought and behaved as if he were a lawyer, and he submitted numerous discovery requests that were designed to overwhelm our office in trying to comply. He sent in this huge discovery request that required my office to produce a mountain of documents that had to be provided to him by a specific date. The request included information Lamar wanted from the Postal Inspection Service. I missed the part that required my office to produce documents and thought the discovery request was just for the inspection service, so I sent the request to them. In his request for documents, Lamar asked for copies of the employee's CA-8s, which were relevant to their claims for compensation.

During the hearing, Lamar asked for sanctions against the Postal Service for failing to comply with a legal discovery request. The administrative judge agreed, sanctioned the Postal Service, and did not allow me to present any CA-8 forms as exhibits during the hearing. Without the CA-8s, the Postal Service's case against the employee could not be supported, and I was in quite a dilemma.

You cannot fathom what happened next. The infamous outhouse lawyer made my case for me. Even though he had requested the CA-8s in discovery, he already had copies of the employee's complete file, which included all his CA-8s. Lamar introduced several exhibits to support his case. However, on cross-examination, I used the same documents submitted by Lamar to question the appellant. Even though I was able to use

Lamar's exhibits, I was not sure how the administrative judge would rule after we were sanctioned.

A month or so later, I was sitting in my office when the morning mail was placed in my box. In it was the long-anticipated arbitration case, and so was the MSPB decision. I was eager and nervous at the same time to read the decisions. This was the first and the last time I would receive two important case decisions on the same day, one based on circumstantial evidence and the other involving being sanctioned for not providing documents during discovery. To my surprise, I had prevailed in both cases, and my reputation as a Postal Service advocate skyrocketed.

After the manager of Human Resources (personnel director) retired, Willie Hathman brought Charlie Amos in from the Southern Region Office on a ninety-day detail. I had previously met Charlie when I went to Memphis for EEO counselor training, and he was the same manager who had invited a group of us over to his home while we were there. Charlie was a very outgoing person, and there was never a dull moment while he was in Fort Worth. He was fun-loving, so we went out several evenings, frequenting every club in the area. And on Saturday mornings, he would get a group of us together to go bowling. Never a dull moment.

Since there was a vacancy in Human Resources, Willie had to select a new manager. The manager's job was a coveted position, and many individuals were interested and applied. Jerry Selmon, who was the former labor representative at Fort Worth, was interested in returning as the manager, and as I understood it, he was a frontrunner for the position based on his knowledge of Fort Worth and of the managers in that office. I am sure Jerry had an advocate in Charles Slaten, the manager of Mail

Processing, whom Wille had recently promoted to manager of Distribution Operations. Charles had been Jerry's counterpart in Personnel when they were the top two managers, under the manager of Human Resources.

After I became aware that Jerry was being considered for the Manager's position, I felt compelled to make Willie aware of the conversation I had overheard between Jerry, who was then the Labor Relations representative, and his newly detailed Labor Relations assistant. Jerry was popping off after the manager of Mail Processing, Leonard Allen, retired, saying that Willie was not qualified to fill the position. I went to Willie and informed him of that conversation. I am not sure if that conversation had a bearing on the process, but Jerry was not selected. Instead, Wille selected the manager of Human Resources from a smaller office out of Baton Rouge, Louisiana, named Joe Bob Clendenin. In my opinion, he was a much better selection—and one that would pay dividends for me later.

While at that training session in Memphis, there was discussion about a new program in which postmasters and other managers could identify promising, younger employees who used employee-assistance services and place them on what was called a fast track. When I returned to Fort Worth, I visited the postmaster's office, talked to him about the program, and asked him if he would consider me when the program was implemented. He stated that he would investigate it.

I did not know it at the time, but Willie wanted me to be the first Black postmaster in the Fort Worth Management Sectional Center. To prepare me, he set me up with a detail to the Weatherford, Texas, post office as the financial officer, where I learned how the financial side of the post office worked. It was a great assignment, and he made sure I was working under a postmaster who was fair. The detail was uneventful other than just learning new things, but there was one very interesting day. While manning the desk right off the window unit there at Weatherford, a customer came in and asked to speak to the postmaster. The clerk at the window informed the customer that the postmaster was not in at that time, adding that the Finance manager was in the back and he could speak with him. The customer came to the back, where I was sitting behind a desk, wearing a suit and tie. Near my desk was a janitor who just happened to be White; he was sweeping the floor and dressed in his janitor uniform. The customer did not say a word to me, instead talking to the janitor to address his concerns. Even after the janitor pointed the customer to me, the customer never said a word to me. The year was 1980 or 1981. What a shame.

A few months later, Willie sent me to the Bridgeport, Texas, post office as officer-in-charge, which is the official title for someone temporarily replacing a postmaster. After reporting to Bridgeport, it did not take me long to realize that there were no Black people living in the town. As a matter of fact, I was driving down the street one day and saw a Black person, but he was someone I knew from Fort Worth. I jumped out of my car to greet him. I had a feeling about being the only Black person in that town, and it led me to believe that I needed to leave Bridgeport before the sun went down. I guess I got caught up in those old sayings about not letting sundown catch you in town. I was determined that no one was going to pin anything on me, because history has taught me that if anything goes wrong, everyone assumes the Black guy did it. It would not happen to me for being in that town after dark.

Bridgeport was an interesting detail, and I learned a lot. However, it did not start out so great. One of the main functions of a postmaster in a small office was to deposit all moneys taken in daily. I was required to reconcile all the financial activities, make sure the books balanced at the end of the day, and make the daily bank deposit. The bank would make sure the deposit was correct and provide a receipt to verify it. On my first bank deposit, the teller informed me that I was a hundred dollars short. Being so new in the position and still inexperienced, I did not know what had happened. I had to trust that the bank clerk had counted the money correctly. The clerk told me that if the hundred dollars showed up at the final reconciliation, she would give me credit. The next day, she said that the account was still a hundred dollars short. I never kept that kind of money on me, so the top clerks in the office volunteered to loan me the money. I went to the bank and made sure the bank deposit was correct, and I reimbursed the clerks the next day. I did not make that mistake again and really got to be pretty good at closing out the office.

While at Bridgeport, I was shocked to learn how many people in that area were receiving food stamps (government assistance for necessities). I had worked my entire career in the Postal Service in the city, and there was a misconception that Black folks were the only people receiving food stamps, or at least that is what some would lead you to believe. I realized that was not so; there were a lot of needy people in rural America.

I soon realized that I had to let Willie down, as there was no way I would become his first Black postmaster. Let me paint a picture of my dilemma. The Fort Worth Management Sectional Center included medium-size post offices in cities around Fort Worth, such as Arlington, Euless, Bedford, Hurst, and Weatherford. Wichita Falls was also in our sectional center and at the time was the second-largest post office under Willie's management structure. Those cities had higher-level positions, and there was no way I could qualify for one of them. Bridgeport and most of the offices I could qualify for were level 18 offices, whereas the ones I mentioned were level 20 and above. All the other post offices were in cities similar in size to Bridgeport— very rural areas where there were little or no Black residents.

In considering a move to one of those rural areas, I knew the position I would place my family in. I had three young boys, and as they got older, they would turn their attention to girls. I could not place my boys in a situation where there were no Black girls and the only choice for them would be White girls. Even though it was in the early eighties, that would not work in rural America, and I would not dare place my boys in that situation. I had to focus my career options in other areas.

## Chapter 13

### Seventh Stage of Going Postal

After being a Labor Relations assistant for a few years, I felt I was ready for the next challenge. I secretly hoped my supervisor would get promoted, which would give me a great opportunity to be selected as the Labor Relations representative. I would become the third person to hold that position since it was established in the Fort Worth post office. However, there was no movement, and I began to get anxious about moving on and getting promoted. I decided to talk to Willie about moving to Customer Service as a supervisor at one of the stations. I was a level 16, and the supervisor positions were level 15. However, I did not have the experience to move right into a level 16 position, which would be an assistant at a very large station or the manager of a very small station. I did not have the experience for either one, so it was determined that I would be assigned to the next best thing. That turned out to be a position at the very station where I had worked my first few years carrying mail and where I had bid for my first carry route.

When I arrived at Berry Street, some of the people I had previously worked with were still there, but most of the old-timers who harbored racist attitudes were no longer there, which was a blessing for me. I did not have to deal with those attitudes.

While assigned at Berry Street, and being a former carrier at the unit, things went along smoothly, and I had very few incidents. However, I did make one of the worst managerial decisions of my postal career. Two carriers got into a altercation, and one came to me and stated that he had been threatened by the other. I called the carrier into the office and began chewing him out. He asked me to hear his side of the story, but I refused. I let him know that his conduct was unacceptable, which it was, but the error I made was not listening to him. I had made an enemy for life.

Saturdays at Berry Street Station were challenging because all the other supervisors and the manager were off, and the supervisor on duty had to open and close, which made for about a twelve-hour day. The time went by so fast, however, that it really was not bad.

One interesting employee who carried mail for me was gay and a fun-loving person who was great to be around because he would say some of the darndest things. Frank was an excellent letter carrier and would always finish his assignments early. On one day when some routes needed help, I instructed Franko, as we called him, to assist another carrier when he returned from his route. Franko forgot, and the next morning I jumped all over him and told him that he had left me hanging the day before. He looked down at my pants and said, "I did?" All I could do was laugh.

After my second assignment at Berry Street, I was assigned to the largest office in the city that had a level 16 supervisory position. I worked there for a short period and was then assigned to Southtown Annex—yes, the second station where I had carried mail. Most of my good friends were still carrying mail there, and I had a new challenge: Could I supervise carriers I knew very well, and would they let me supervise them?

After reporting to the station, most of the Black carriers who were there when I carried mail readily accepted me as their manager. A few other carriers had not been there when I worked there, but that did not cause any concern initially.

The person I had begun carrying mail with back in 1967, Van Malone, was still there, as was an aspiring 204-B acting supervisor I used occasionally when the regular supervisor was off. Willie Jones and Lewis Childress were still there, but the one who was most difficult to supervise was the one I called Pops. He could not get to work on time and took too much time delivering his mail. There was another carrier named Don Caldwell, whom I knew very well from my childhood, that I will speak about later. The other carriers were not any problem— well, except for one. More on that later.

A younger carrier who worked there was out due to an injury, but I had met him while I was attending TCJC. One day, while attending a football game on the campus where my oldest son was playing, I noticed him on the sideline. Not really meaning anything, I walked up to him and asked when he would be returning to work. He did not like my question and became very irate. One of his friends had to hold him back to prevent the possibility of his attacking me. I stood there looking at him just like the fool he was making of himself, knowing that if he had engaged me in a fight—win, lose, or draw—he would be fired. I thought he was out of his mind.

A few weeks later, he came to the office and, as if he were a politician, walked around greeting all the carriers. When I saw him, I was very busy and could not engage him. So when I had the opportunity, I asked him if he was reporting for duty, and he told me he was not. I told him to get out of my office and explained that anytime he came to the office for any reason other than reporting for duty, he had to have my permission to enter. He stepped outside the door and began to curse me. I walked up to where he was and asked if he was talking to me, and he abruptly left. A few weeks later, he reported for duty and turned out to be one of the nicest carriers you would want to meet.

Another incident that I found humorous involved a little, fat letter carrier I knew from the days I had carried mail at Southtown. He was a likable person even though he had some racist beliefs. After the Martin Luther King Jr. holiday was established, which became a federal holiday, the carrier told me he was not going to celebrate it. I told him that he could bring his little fat ass to work, but the rest of us were going to take off. He could not do anything but laugh.

One carrier in the office was also there when I carried mail; he was the one whom the manager asked me to assist and I said, "Hell, no." The carrier was not liked by anyone in the office, and I just knew I was going to have problems with him. But I was determined to find a way to get to him, to see what made him tick. One morning I noticed something about him, and I set out to explore it. Southtown Annex was not your standard station, and businesses in the area, as well as some regular customers, would come by to pick up their mail. One morning a female customer from his route came, asked for him, and asked to get her mail early. When he went to the front to meet the lady to give her her mail, I noticed a gleam in his eyes, seeming to show a side of him I had not previously seen. After he came back to his workstation, I took a chance and said something to him that would either make him angry or make him laugh. I told him it was no wonder he could not finish his route in a timely manner because he was out there flirting with the women. He smiled and assured me that was not the case. The ice was broken.

I had a newfound friend. Several days, this carrier would stay after all the other carriers had left the office, and we would just talk. He was really a delight to talk with, and I discovered that he was a very intelligent person. We struck up an after-hours relationship of which the carriers who detested him remained unaware.

On Saturday mornings, we started a practice of not assigning anyone to a route, and then we would split it among those carries who finished early due to businesses on their routes being closed or just not having very much mail to deliver. On this particular Saturday morning, I went to each carrier and gave him or her mail that I wanted delivered. One carrier basically refused, saying he would carry the mail as soon as I got Harris, my new friend, to carry a swing. I was just about to jack this carrier up for failing to follow my instructions, but before I could say anything, my good friend and 204-B acting supervisor, who was working in the adjacent workstation, stated that no one ever instructs Harris to carry swings. To show up the 204-B and to gain my authority in the office, I walked over to Harris with a swing of mail, not knowing how he would respond to me, and I told him that when he finished his route, I needed him to deliver this swing of mail. Harris loudly replied, "Okay, boss!" You could have heard a feather drop to the floor. I did not have a problem with any of the carriers I directed from that point on when it came to carrying swings of mail.

One carrier in the office was impossible for me to reach. He was just inherently slow or lazy. Every morning, no matter the amount of mail he had, he would request overtime to complete his route. The volume of mail he had for most days would not require overtime from other carriers to complete the route. I got tired of confronting him daily, so I decided I would accompany him on his route for a week, first to see if he needed the overtime he was requesting, which I believed he did not, and second, to hopefully fix in his mind that he could carry his assignment without needing overtime. Each day we went out, he came back early, except for the two days a week he had full coverage. And even on those days he did not need the amount of overtime he had been requesting. Saturday was consistently a very light mail day, so overtime was never needed.

After spending the week with him, I brought him into the office and explained what I had observed. I told him which days he would possibly need overtime and which days he would not. On the very first Saturday after speaking with him, he approached my desk with a request for overtime—and I lost it. I told him I was not authorizing any overtime for him and directed him to go back to his case. I expected him to finish his route in eight hours. I noticed him talking to the carrier who worked next to him, Don Caldwell, who had recently been selected as the office's shop steward for the upcoming year and whom I had known for most of my life because he had lived next door to me when I was a child. He was about four years older than I was, and I always looked up to him like a big brother. Don felt obligated to take up the carrier's complaint and asked if he could speak with me.

As Don approached my desk, he summoned the carrier and the current shop steward to accompany him. I stopped them. I told Don that I had agreed to speak with him, but the others had to remain working. Don did not like this and basically challenged my authority. When it appeared there would be no constructive conversation, I instructed Don to return to work. He looked at me and asked, "Are you a fool?" I tried to keep my cool for several reasons. One, I did not want him to get in trouble, so I once again instructed him to return to work, ignoring what he said. He refused to follow my instructions, and since I was trained in labor relations, I knew the steps to take. I gave him a direct order to return to work, and he again refused. I then instructed him to leave the premises, and he again refused. But my next comment got his attention. I believe he realized he was in trouble when I told him that I would be calling the Postal Inspection Service to have him removed from the premises. I noticed the look on his face and as he was preparing to leave. Just then, the guy I respected most in the office, Willie Jones, who was also a good friend of Don's, came over and asked me if we could talk about the situation. Since he was one of my favorite people in the entire post office, I agreed. We went into my office, and I lit into Don. I told him that he was doing his job as a carrier, and I could not believe he would put his job on the line trying to help a carrier who was too sorry to do his job. After a few words from my trusted friend, I decided I would give Don a break. I told him that I would not take any actions against him under one condition. The next morning, after all the carriers reported, I needed him to stand in the middle of the workroom floor and apologize to me. He was to place everyone else on notice that they were not to even get close to the behavior he had displayed. He agreed and did as instructed. I believe I got more mileage out of not firing him than I would have if I had. As a matter of fact, several of the young carriers came to me and commended me on the way I had handled the situation. I did not have any disciplinary problems from that point, and I was greatly relieved when the carrier with whom I was having delivery and overtime problems bid out of the station.

One problem that I discovered at Southtown was that the mail volume in previous years had not been counted correctly, especially by my predecessor. I counted the mail accurately and, based on the low volume, realized I was using too many hours to get the mail delivered. The manager before me had inflated the volume and was claiming hours similar to what I was using with the lower, accurate volume. I was getting jumped on by my managers daily and accused of being inefficient. When we attended manager meetings, I was ostracized for raising the issue about the inflated mail count. I knew that it was not good to throw pervious managers under the bus, but I felt that if I was going to be constantly chewed out, I was going to tell the truth about what was going on.

The managers downtown did not care much for me, and I knew it. They tested me by transferring the Special Delivery Unit from the managers at the main office to Southtown Annex under my supervision. One reason the unit was being moved was that the special delivery carrier craft director was a handful, and they did not know how to deal with him. He was a Black New Yorker who consistently caused them headaches.

I was aware of his reputation, so after the unit reported to the office, I tried to rein him in. One of my first opportunities to reach out to him was when one of the special delivery carriers called in sick, and I did not have a clue about the territory or how I would cover the vacancy. I went to the craft director and told him I needed his help. He took charge and divided the mail up between the other carriers, and the problem was resolved. Believe it or not, just showing him a little respect was all I needed to do.

However, a problem ensued. The craft director was assigned a special delivery item that was not correctly addressed, so he did not deliver it. I believed he knew where the business was and could have delivered it, but I had no way to prove it. Prior to moving to Southtown, the special delivery carriers were required to take undelivered mail to the main office. In this case, he returned the special delivery item he was unable to deliver. As I stated, he was not liked, and when the supervisor at the main office saw the returned special deliver, he reported it to his manager. The manager told him to call me and tell me to suspend the special delivery carrier for not delivering the mail. When I got the call from the supervisor, who was an acting supervisor, it did not sit well with me. As a former Labor Relations employee, I knew that discipline was not to be dictated by someone else. Others can suggest discipline after an investigation is conducted, but they cannot dictate it. I told the acting supervisor that I would investigate the situation, and if I determined that disciplinary action was appropriate, I would issue it. I called the carrier over and asked him if he had the mail item, and he indicated that he did. I then asked him why he had not delivered it, and he replied that there was no such address. I asked whether he knew where the business was located, and he informed me that he did not. I had no way of proving that what he said was not the truth. When he asked me if he was going to be disciplined—because he had heard at the main office that he would be—I informed him that he would not. When I next spoke to the acting supervisor, I told him to tell his manager that I did not have any proof that the carrier had failed to do his job and would not be issuing discipline.

# Chapter 14

## Eighth Stage of Going Postal

Things did not get any better at the station to which I was assigned, and I was getting antsy about my career. I saw an advertisement for ad-hoc EEO investigators that I believed I was qualified for, and the position was an EAS-19. I would receive a boost in pay if I was hired for the position.

After applying, I went to Memphis for an interview. My Labor Relations background proved valuable, and I was selected for the position. I returned to Memphis later for a three-week training, and once that was completed, I was assigned to conduct EEO investigations in Houston.

I encountered one problem, though. I had not spoken to Willie about my intentions. He found out through the grapevine, and he was not pleased. Afterward, when he would see me at the post office, he would walk in another direction.

My EEO investigative assignment required me to travel to Houston and conduct investigations one week, and the next week I would write my investigative report. There was no space in the Fort Worth office, so I was approved to work from home. That was a very eerie feeling, especially on those weeks when I had very little to do because I had resolved all or most of the cases assigned to me.

I performed EEO investigation for about a year, but I knew it was basically a dead-end street. I had to get back to Station and Branches. When I returned to Operations, I was assigned to work for a very good friend of mine, James Conley, who was the first Black manager over Station and Branches in Fort Worth.

Speaking of James, he was promoted to Mail Processing prior to my going to Maintenance. He had been a letter carrier, as I had, and he had a bright future. However, like me, he met with a few roadblocks that prevented him from rising as quickly as he should have. I was in Willie's office one day when he was on the telephone with the director of Customer Services, and he was asking why James would get rave reviews anytime he applied for a job in an office outside Fort Worth, but when he applied in Fort Worth, he could not get selected for a manager's job. After Willie had been on board a few years, James's career finally took off.

I was assigned to Benbrook Station in Benbrook, Texas, as the manager of the level 16 station. James was not sure what kind of manager I was, and initially he was kind of hands-on. But he soon turned me loose to manage the station. Benbrook was an easy station to manage, and I found many areas where improvements could be made.

Each morning when I arrived, I would greet each carrier at his or her workstation and engage in some small talk. Some of the carriers did not need any motivation and went about doing their jobs as required. One such carrier reminded me of the old saying, "Do not judge a book by its cover." I know now that I was wrong to think this, but the carrier looked every bit a

Klansman. But to my pleasant surprise, he was one of the nicest carriers in the office. One morning as I was making my rounds, he said to me, "Hello, sunshine." I knew what he meant, but I quickly replied, "What did you call me?" He got nervous and asked me if something was wrong. I laughed and told him nothing was wrong; I was just pulling his leg. However, I took the opportunity to tell him a story about White people calling Black Americans names that referred to their skin color or character in reverse. He was apologetic, but I assured him it was not necessary.

However, I inherited quite possibly the dumbest supervisor in the Fort Worth post office. In looking at the Saturday schedule, I noticed that this supervisor had three part-time flexible (PTF) carriers reporting on Saturday without an assignment. I asked him why, and his answer was that he was not letting a "sub" off on a Saturday. I asked him what he was planning to have them do, and he stated he would find something for them to do. Now this is what I mean by dumb: each office's performance is measured by how many work hours they put in versus the mail volume for the day. PTFs were guaranteed at least two hours every time they were scheduled, whether you needed them or not. I had to take over scheduling the carriers, and in doing so, I allowed people who wanted to take a Saturday off to take it, and I would then schedule a PTF to cover the vacant route. I was determined not to have carriers standing around waiting on work.

After being at Benbrook for some time, I had made several improvements, and the office was being run efficiently. I was instructed to have the office closed out by 5:30 p.m. each day, which included balancing all the financial transactions for the day. I was not going to rush on such an important assignment, so I would clock out after working eight hours and remain in the office, taking my time to ensure there were no errors in my paperwork.

A level 18 office job was advertised, and I applied. I was running one of the most efficient offices in the city, including all the higher-level offices, and I thought I would be a shoo-in for the position. I was the only level 16 manager running a Finance and Carrier Unit in the city. James Conley had to evaluate my performance at Benbrook. He would be accused of favoritism if he let anything personal surface in his evaluation of my performance, so all he did was compare my year-to-date stats against those of the prior year to show how efficiently I was running the office. He did not include one word in his evaluation that was not supported by my record.

Before long, I learned that I had not been recommended for the next level because I allegedly did not have enough experience. However, I also found out that two White level 15 supervisors had been recommended. I asked why they had been recommended when I was not, and my supposed lack of experience was cited again. However, the two who were recommended did not run their own units as I did, and they basically assisted their managers. I, on the other hand, ran my own office and had demonstrated the ability to run an efficient station. Something was not right.

I had gotten back in Willie's good graces, and even though I did not like what I felt I had to do, I went to him and explained the unfairness I had just experienced. Willie was never one to let people know what he was thinking, and the first thing he asked me was whether I had spoken to the manager over

Customer Services. I replied that I had not, so he suggested that I do that. I did not want to go to the manager because I felt that my not getting the job was the result of a concerted effort by the Customer Service managers. The manager who stated I was not qualified or ready for promotion had been brought to the Fort Worth office by the manager with whom Willie wanted me to speak. Despite my misgivings, I made an appointment to speak with him, and we had a decent conversation. He reviewed my evaluations and could not disagree that I had performed efficiently, and he promised me that he would personally review any future application I submitted. Before I left his office, the manager had one more thing to tell me, which I believe had a twofold purpose. One was to get me out of Customer Services so he and his managers would not have to deal with me, and the second was that he probably knew I would jump at the opportunity. He informed me that the Labor Relations representative for whom I had previously worked was getting a promotion to the Southern Region Office, so the position in Human Resources would soon be posted for application. That was good news, and even though I felt I had been mistreated, going back to Labor Relations would be like going home.

Prior to the position's being posted, I had to go to Washington, DC for three weeks of training related to my current position. The Labor Relations position was posted while I was there, but I did not realize it. James Conley called and asked me if I had seen it because, to the best of my understanding, Willie had told him about it and wanted me to apply.

I applied for the position, and my main competition would have been my successor as a Labor Relations assistant, but she opted to apply for a level 18 manager of Training position, whereas the Labor job was a level 19. I never found out why she opted for the other position, but it paid off for her later, when she was promoted to manager of Human Resources in Mobile, Alabama. Regardless, she was out of my way, and I was basically guaranteed the position. I interviewed with the manager I spoke of earlier, Joe Bob Clendenin, and came to believe that he had already made up his mind based on my prior performance as his Labor Relations assistant.

Shortly after returning to Benbrook Station, I received a call from none other than Willie Hathman. He said, "Young man, how did your interview go?" All I could say was that it had gone well, even though it was not much of an interview. I felt I had the job in the bag because I was not asked many questions. I also had a sneaking suspicion that he and my boss-to-be, Joe Bob, had decided I would get the position long before I reported for the interview.

# Chapter 15

## Ninth Stage of Going Postal

### Home at Last

I do not regret leaving Human Resources for the four years I was out, but in looking back on my tenure as a supervisor and as a manager of Customer Services, plus the year I worked as an EEO investigator, I realized I had gained valuable experience that would serve me well in my new position as Labor Relations representative.

However, I would have to overcome several hurdles before I would truly be home. The first problem I encountered was selecting a Labor Relations assistant. In my absence, the previous Labor Relations Representative had detailed a former nemesis of mine to assist him. The person had also been the clerk craft director with the local American Postal Workers Union. When I arrived, he was still assigned to the assistant position, so I continued using him until the position was formerly advertised. But since he was doing a good job, I selected him for the Labor Relations assistant position. There was a little unrest, however, because he had applied for the Labor Relations Representative position, and some of the Hispanics in the office felt that he should have gotten the position because he was currently working in the office. Most of those who felt that way, however, were unaware of my years in Labor Relations and the reputation that I had developed.

I had one more hurdle to overcome. I had thought I would walk right back into the job and start where I had left off four years earlier. But I was in for a rude awakening. It took me a while to get my feet under me and to command the respect I had prior to leaving.

I quickly realized that my predecessor had not been big on challenging the higher-level managers who ran Operations, either on the Customer Service side or on the Mail Processing side. I ran into a few buzzsaws. One of the strongest managers in the building was over Customer Services. He was the one who had promised me that he would review my applications while I was still under his management team. However, now I had to deal with him on any decisions I made or wanted to make as the Labor Relations representative. True to form, one of my first challenges came from him shortly after I returned to Labor. I was trying to explain that one of his managers had made a contractual violation, and the first thing he said was, "Where is that in the contract?" I was still settling in so I might not have responded as strongly as I wanted to. I was not intimidated by him, but I was not as sure in my position as I should have been. It took me a while to develop the trust from the operational managers that I indeed knew what I was talking about and that I could back it up with regulations or contractual citations.

The Fort Worth office was growing, and we were taking on new territory. I needed someone to assist in Labor Relations, and I selected a person who had just completed a management-training program and was looking for a position. This person would eventually become my right hand and a very close friend as time went on.

However, things got off to rocky start. Shortly after bringing him on, I was on a detail to the manager of Employee Relations position, so I was trying to learn that job and train a new person at the same time. My patience was not what it should have been, and I found myself getting frustrated with my trainee. I would give him a set of instructions, but he would not tell me that he did not fully understand what I was asking of him. Instead, he would go to the Labor Relations assistant for clarification. Well, that information got back to me, and after a month or so, I called the Labor Relations assistant in and told him I was terminating this person's training. My assistant asked if he could work with the trainee a little longer, and I agreed. That was a great suggestion on his part and a great decision on my part.

The trainee was William Jackson, and he had great credentials. He held two master's degrees, and he was a retired army major and a recipient of the Silver Star for valor while serving in Vietnam. He was also a very levelheaded person. When I was authorized to fill another Labor Relations assistant position, I told him that if he made the top three during the interview process, I would select him. Unbeknownst to me, my boss had plans to offer the position to a woman out of the Dallas office. I guessed he was looking to increase diversity. However, I had made a promise to Bill Jackson, and I was not going back on my word. I selected Bill, and over time he became the best advocate in the office. In fact, he received recognition for winning over twenty cases in one year. The only reason he did better than I had was that I was not taking on as many cases since I had more assistants (smile). I got to be a little jealous of Bill mainly because I had built very good relationships with the arbitrators on our local panel over the years, but after he came on, the arbitrators would always ask me how Bill was doing when I presented a case. He was a great addition to the office.

We continued growing, and I needed to fill one more position. There were several applicants, and among them was one young White woman whom I had detailed to handle grievances in the Arlington post office. Another great candidate from the Dallas Bulk Mail Center had assisted in handling grievances. His name was John Merit, which will be mentioned later.

John and the White woman were in the top three, and John was the best interviewee. I had to decide. John was Black, and at the time I had a Hispanic man and a Black man on my staff. I was concerned about appearances, so in order to bring about a more diverse staff, I selected the White woman. Initially, things rocked along well, but later she began to cause me some concern. She started raising issues about the men in the office going to lunch together and not inviting her. I was old school and did not feel comfortable with White women being in the company of Black men. I had gone to lunch with white women in my career, and the stares were a little much for me and made me very uncomfortable. As a matter of fact, we had a meeting in Fort Worth at a local hotel, and after the meeting a group of us went out for drinks, which was not unusual. The attractive White woman who worked in the personnel office told me that, before I left to go home, she wanted to dance. I agreed, even though I was still not comfortable. As if to validate my concerns, one of the postal employees who was not with our specific group but was there after our meeting ended saw me dancing with her and said loudly, "A Black guy dancing with a White girl!" He was so loud that I worried about the possibility of some redneck having objections. I did not like the attention, so after we finished the dance, I got the hell out of Dodge.

Back to my new Labor Relations assistant. I explained to her that we were not deliberately excluding her from lunches and made her aware of how Black men felt about being in the company of only White women on what could appear to be a lunch date. She did not accept my explanation and was openly unhappy working in the office.

Several months later, she came to me about an opportunity for promotion and asked my opinion. I encouraged her to apply; as I recall, it was a position of the same level or a hybrid position that allowed her to be promoted to a higher level. She applied and was accepted.

I posted the Labor Relations assistant position, and some of the same people who had previously applied did so again, including John Merritt. I knew I would be faced with the same dilemma, and I discussed my concerns with my friend James Conley. He asked me to look across the atrium we were in and tell him what I saw. What I saw were offices with nothing but White people. He then asked me if I believed they were truly concerned about how diverse their offices appeared to be. I knew the answer. I knew or at least believed that White people do not put that burden on themselves; they select the best qualified, or at least whomever they desire. I decided to select John Merritt, and I never looked back.

After selecting John, I held a staff meeting. At that time, the staff consisted of three Blacks and a Hispanic in Fort Worth and a White Labor assistant in Lubbock, whom I had inherited when Fort Worth took over the Panhandle offices. We also had one White and one Black secretary. I made the group aware that eyes would be on our office as we were the majority minority labor staff in our region. I told them that we could not be just good; we had to be the best. In looking back on our efforts, I see that we might not have been the best every time during our grading period, but we were consistently in the upper echelon and received recognition for that. One of the procedures I implemented was to have one of my staff members assign arbitration cases. I decided to do that to prevent what had happened to me from happening again. I did not want to appear to be cherry-picking cases. I instructed my labor representative that I would take the most difficult cases, including removal cases.

During this period, we seemed to be invaded by people from the Chicago post office who were coming in either on details or into permanent positions. One young lady did not have anything good to say about Black people in the South. She was Black and frequently bragged about the accomplishments of Black employees in Chicago. She talked about the Black postmaster from Chicago who had become the Southern Region manager, bragging about how much earlier he had been the postmaster in Chicago and saying that the Fort Worth office had only recently promoted a Black person to postmaster. She told a group of us Blacks that Southern Blacks were too passive and did not fight to move up. I grew tired of her comments, and I decided to give her a little history lesson along with a reality check. I made her aware that, in the South, White people, especially those without an education, held higher-level positions in the Postal Service because jobs were not as plentiful elsewhere, especially with the pay they were receiving, which was a good wage in the South. I told her more Black people worked at post offices in the North because White people had better jobs elsewhere and chose not to work at the post office. I explained that it stands to reason that Black employees would excel in places like Chicago because of the system of promoting from within, which would lead to more Black managers. I further explained that, when I finally broke in, there were only a handful of Black managers in Fort Worth because the good-ol'-boy system was in place and it took time to change that system. It had nothing to do with Black people in the South not being aggressive or being slow. I enjoyed giving her a little something to think about and get her off her high horse.

While working in Labor Relations, I developed good working relationships with most of the supervisors and managers, and in talking with Maintenance managers, I learned that they were hiring custodians. Around that time, a good friend from church, Jesse Jones, had told me that he was looking for a change. He was working for the housing authority but was not able to make any moves to better himself. I knew that he had several two-year degrees from what was then TCJC and that he would be a good fit for the Postal Service since the work he was doing at the housing authority was similar to several job functions at the Postal Service. I shared the openings with him, and I told him that, as a veteran with his background, he should be able to get on without any problem. The only issue was that he had to come on as a part-time employee, but that status should not extend past six months. I added that he would not have to work as a custodian for long based on his background and the work he performed at the housing authority. I felt there was a good possibility he could be promoted within months of becoming full-time. Jesse trusted me and took the job, and about six months in he became a full-time mechanic. A year or so later, he became a supervisor in Maintenance, where he was over all the building equipment maintenance for the small post offices in our cluster or management structure. If I did nothing else good during my tenure, I was most proud that things worked out so well for Jesse.

The Postal Service went through a restructuring, and the Fort Worth office fell under the newly established Dallas division, which meant that my office would be under the jurisdiction of the Dallas Labor Relations. That did not cause any concerns, though, and the manager in Dallas did not bother or interfere with how I ran Labor Relations in Fort Worth.

Periodically, the Labor Relations manager in Dallas, whose name was Delward Stracner, would ask me to accompany him in visiting some office under the Fort Worth umbrella. So when I was set to conduct a training session in Wichita Falls, he accompanied me. Del had friends everywhere and said he wanted to visit a couple who lived outside Wichita Falls. Then he told me something that would make the visit to these people probably the most interesting visit of my life.

He told me that we would have dinner at the couple's home, and he warned me to not get alarmed if I heard the lady talk about her grandson, who went by—you will not believe it— "Nigger Bob!" Yep, the boy was called Nigger Bob. Del asked me not to be offended. I told him I would be okay.

After the training class, which Del slept through, we struck out to visit his friends. I was not sure where we were going, but we soon pulled into a trailer park. I knew I was in trouble. The area did not look right to me, this being my first-ever trip to a trailer park. We went in to meet the homeowners, and after pleasantries, the lady served us dinner. She was polite and treated me fine. I thought I would be a little uneasy eating there, but the dinner went off without incident. As a matter of fact, she was a pretty good cook. I do not recall the sides, but she served steak and it was delicious.

After dinner, she served beer, and then it happened—she mentioned that Nigger Bob was coming over later. She had a unique explanation for why the child was called Nigger Bob. In her explanation, which I also found to be racist, she said that when Nigger Bob was a baby, his mother had carried him on her hip, you guessed it, like colored women did. I could not wait to get out of there, but Del was not ready to leave. So we went outside and had a few more beers. While outside, a friend of the family came and drank with us. I do not recall how the conversation ended up on him, but I soon realized he was fresh out of prison and his favorite pastime was using his knife on those with whom he had disputes. I made sure not to add anything to the conversation that would set him off, but that was still not enough for me to be comfortable in the setting. I kept my eyes on him until I could get the hell out of there.

When the new division structure was established, Willie Hathman was appointed as the division manager over the Oklahoma division, and he later became the division manager of the Dallas division. Later, there was another restructuring, and the Fort Worth office became a district that was no longer responsible to Dallas. Dallas was a district like Fort Worth, but Dallas was also the home of the newly established Area Office. The restructuring resulted in new positions being created, and some of us were grandfathered into newly generated positions. My position was elevated to manager of Labor Relations, and the Labor Relations assistants were elevated to Labor Relations representatives. I received a promotion from level 19 to level 21 initially, but it was changed later to level 22. All former Labor Relations assistants were promoted to representatives at level 19.

With the restructuring came new challenges. We had a new district manager, and he brought in a new staff to which we had to adjust. Early on, there was a confrontation with one of the new managers. As part of a process, when adverse action was requested against a manager, the requesting manager was required to let the accused state his or her side of the story, take notes on the meeting, and make recommendations to Labor Relations with the notes of the meeting. Labor Relations would then prepare the disciplinary action, following precise regulations. In this case, this new manager sent what he thought was the disciplinary action for my office to type up. I called his office and attempted to advise him of what was required to process the discipline, and he went into a tirade. He told me he was f---ing tired of people telling him what he needed to do and then hung up on me. Needless to say, I was foaming at the mouth, and I came very close to going over to his office to set him straight. But I thought better of it and went to my boss, Joe Bob, instead, still fuming. I told Joe Bob that if he did not go over to the guy's office and straighten him out, I would put my job on the line because I was not going to put up with anything like that. Job Bob asked me what had happened, and after I explained, he stood up, threw his glasses on the desk, and shot across the hall to confront this manager. Job Bob and this manager were on the district manager's staff, so he did not have to deal with protocol. A few minutes later, Job Bob returned and told me that the manager had his door locked so he could not get in to see him. While we were talking, the manager walked up and, before we could say anything to him, apologized for his conduct. However, that did not stop Joe Bob from lighting into his butt. When Joe Bob finished with him, I got right in his face and told him one thing—I was a man. I am not sure if he understood the full ramifications of what I was saying, however. I later found out he was going around saying he found out who was really running the Fort Worth office. His assessment was wrong, but he did find out that Human Resource types were not going to be bullied or run over by Operation managers. I did not have that problem with that manager again.

The restructuring also provided us with a very cocky manager of Mail Processing whose favorite saying was that the tail does not wag the dog, referring to Human Resources' being a support unit to Operations. One thing this manager did not understand, as most Operations managers did, was that we, and especially Labor Relations, dealt with regulations and contractual language they could not rewrite. Eventually they would have to conform. For example, a manager came to my office and said that she needed to excess (get rid of) clerks from her unit. The process called for her to justify the need to downsize, and the clerks would then be sent to Mail Processing as unassigned regulars, where most clerks resided. The Mail Processing manager got ticked off when he found out that he was gaining additional full-time clerks that he did not need, so he came to my office raising Cain. He requested that the other manager come to my office as well so we could get the situation straightened out. I quickly made him aware that my job in this instance was to advise the manager on the steps needed to excess clerks from her unit, so he did not need to talk to me. If he had a problem with the decision, he needed to talk with the other manager. He did not like my answer, but he politely left my office.

Many interesting grievance-arbitration issues arose during my later years in Labor Relations. One of the weirdest issues that came about started with a case being presented in arbitration by Bill Jackson. While beginning his presentation in a removal case, which was based on a last-chance agreement, the arbitrator told Bill that he did not believe in last-chance agreements. Bill came to my office, told me what the arbitrator had said, and explained the danger of putting the employee back to work. To clarify, we would place an employee on a last-chance agreement between the union and Labor Relations to allow the employee one last chance to show that he or she could follow regulations and be a productive employee. I went over to talk to the arbitrator and questioned him about his position on last-chance agreements. He told me, "Mr. Hargis, either you can put the grievant back to work, or I will." He did not leave any room for negotiation. What was weird about the arbitrator's decision was that he placed the employee on a conditional return to duty, which required the employee's attendance to be acceptable for a specified period— in essence, a last-chance agreement.

Our office set out to review the employee's attendance to ensure compliance. About a month or so later, the floor supervisor made our office aware that the employee was a no-show during a payday weekend. A few days later, the employee walked into my office and presented a medical report that indicated he had been hospitalized for several days after a car had fallen on him while he was working beneath it. In looking at the documentation and determining that it appeared on its surface to be a legitimate document, I decided he could return to work without penalty. I was thinking about how strange the incident was, but I felt it was not sufficient to fire him over or did not breach the agreement the arbitrator had authored.

A month or so later, on another payday weekend, this employee was missing from work again. We knew his absence this time would result in his being removed from the Postal Service. The employee walked into my office once again and provided documentation that on the surface appeared to be legitimate. The document was a police report stating that, on this given day, this individual had been walking down the street when some guys in a pickup truck drove up next to him, grabbed him, hit him in the head, threw him in the bed of the truck, took him to an abandoned house, took him inside, and tied him up, where he remained for three days. Based on the document being a police report, I believed there was nothing we could do, even though the story seemed awfully strange. After the employee left, the other labor representative came into my office, and we were musing over the latest fiasco presented. In going over the story given us, the labor rep said, "I have heard that story before." I asked him what he meant. He went to the file cabinet, pulled the employee's discipline file, and pulled out a police report dated approximately a year earlier that gave the same story.

We soon realized that this employee would go to great lengths to cover up his attendance problems. Knowing the same thing could not have happened the same way, especially almost a year to day after the first incident, I called the employee to my office and showed him the two police reports. I told him that he had the option to resign or wait for a removal action to be taken. He did the smart thing and resigned.

Several changes were taking place in our management structure, and we had our first Hispanic district director assigned at Fort Worth. He was an inspiration to our Hispanic employees, as Willie Hathman was to the Black employees when he was promoted to postmaster. This director's stay was uneventful, except for one notable incident. We were celebrating Black History Month, and we had invited one of the local Black judges, Marylyn Hicks, to speak to a group of employees. She made a beautiful presentation about Black accomplishments in the country, and she never mentioned sports or the entertainment field. The district manager came in to close out the event and make a few comments. What he had to say was shocking. He stood at the podium and stated, "Thank God for the NFL and the NBA." He may have added some other words, but that statement stuck with me as it was totally out of place and very demeaning, especially following the judge's presentation. I drove the judge back to her office, and while on the way, she said, "I started to slap your district manager." She was so upset that all the district manager could think to say was that Blacks excelled in sports.

I was fortunate to have traveled around the Postal Service's Southern Region and made several trips to Washington, DC. At one point, a Labor Relations meeting was scheduled in Biloxi, Mississippi, and initially I was trying to figure why. I traveled to Biloxi with the manager of Labor Relations from Dallas and an area Labor Relations specialist from Dallas. We flew into New Orleans, rented a car, and drove to Biloxi, and we had a very interesting experience on our trip from New Orleans to Biloxi.

I should mention that the trip included three Black guys. I was not very familiar with the area where we were traveling, and we stopped for gas and snacks and to use the restroom. The manager from Dallas was about my age, and the Labor Specialist from the Area Office was a few years younger. The younger person went to the counter to ask the location of the restroom, and the clerk replied, "I just told your father where the restroom was." The guy almost lost it because the clerk had assumed the other guy with us was his father even though they did not look anything alike and their ages were within ten years of each other. The younger guy was so upset by the clerk's comments that he went outside and started to get in the wrong vehicle. As we were leaving the service station, we made the wrong turn and ended up in an area near the Gulf with a lot of abandoned tin buildings, old cars, and boats. We did not see anybody, but the area looked very scary; all I could think about was the movie Deliverance. If you recall the movie, you may understand my fear and concerns.

On another trip to New Orleans in the early days when I was a Labor Relations assistant, I had a great time when I hooked up with another HR type who knew his way around New Orleans. He took me to a club, and we had a ball. The club was different from anything I had seen before. It had an open-air section in the middle where they were serving crabs. I had to get a crash course on how to eat crabs and not eat what they called the dead man. That was interesting. For the rest of the night, we danced and just had a good time. On the way back home, I was with Joe Bob Clendenin and Allen Saul, who were my manager and supervisor, respectively. We were at the airport and decided to eat oysters. I had never eaten oysters before, and just as I placed the oyster on a cracker and started to bite it, both Joe Bob and

Allen told me not to bite it but to place the whole oyster in my mouth. Later I realized that, more than likely, I would not have been able to bite the oyster in two, as I was attempting. They laughed at my attempt. Well, I learned.

A separate trip to New Orleans for a labor meeting gave us the opportunity to stay in a plush hotel called the Royal Orleans, which was right on corner of Bourbon Street and Orleans. I always felt guilty staying in some of the nicer places without my wife, but I made the best of it. The next morning, prior to our meeting, the hotel provided a continental breakfast of fruit and pastries. As we were preparing for our meeting, we noticed a couple coming in and helping themselves to the breakfast. Most of us just sat there wondering who these people were, but good old Delward Stracner knew they did not belong with our group and told them to get the hell out of there. It was rather funny, and they got the hell out of there. Later that night, a group of us explored Bourbon Street, had a few drinks, and took in the sights. As we were walking down the street, I was beckoned by one of the ladies on the street, and initially I was not sure she was beckoning for me. So dumb me pointed at myself in a gesture to ask whether she was directing her attention at me. I don't know if I would have gone over to see what she wanted, but before I could make a move, one of the ladies in our group stated, "I would not go over there if I were you." I asked her what she meant, and she added, "That's not a woman." Believe me, I could not tell, but either way, I did not go. We spent the rest of the night just taking in the sights.

On the last trip to New Orleans, I participated in training sessions to learn about the Family Medical Leave Act, and I was to be in New Orleans for the entire week. The good part was that I was able to take my wife with me, and second good part was that a young lady participating in the training was a native of New Orleans. She knew all the great places to eat, and each night we went to a different restaurant. I have never in my life eaten better food over a period of one week—the greatest food in America.

Speaking of great food, I was introduced to a dish called étouffé on a trip to a little city outside Houston when the Fort Worth labor staff attended a meeting in Houston. The group included me, Bill Jackson, Oscar Ochoa, and John Merritt. John had a sister who lived in LaPorte, Texas, and they were both originally from a city near Shreveport, Louisiana. So they were well schooled in New Orleans–type dishes. John told us that his sister had invited us over for dinner. We did not have a clue as to what we were about to experience. His sister was a beautiful lady inside and out. She was a gracious host, but the best was yet to come. When we were called to dinner, we were presented with a dish that included rice and shrimp—huge shrimp—and we also had fried catfish. The rice and shrimp would have been great alone, but I was introduced to étouffé, with a breathtaking sauce. I had never had a dish like that in my life. I know I embarrassed myself and ate more than my body could hold, but I got it down. I am not sure I thanked John and his sister enough. That was a night I will always remember.

I also attended a labor meeting in Atlanta, Georgia. I went to the main office and realized that most of the people working in the Atlanta main office were Black, which really surprised me. The only other office I had gotten the opportunity to visit that had majority minority employees was the New Orleans office, before the flooding of Hurricane Katrina. In fact, New

Orleans was called the chocolate city at one time. The only thing about the trip to Atlanta that stood out occurred when we were leaving. Our meeting ended early, and we had an opportunity to catch an early flight, but we had to get to the airport quickly and change our flights. One of the guys in our group was the manager over Labor Relations in the Area Office. When we arrived at the airport, the manager rushed through the airport. We thought he was rushing to the gate, but he was not. We were trying to keep up with him, but we soon realized he was headed to the airline hospitality room because he was a member. He was rushing to get a drink, and it was only ten in the morning. It was free, after all. When in Rome …

Toward the end of my postal career, I was involved in several key arbitration cases. The first I recall was a Wichita Falls case. What was unique about this case was the arbitrator assigned to it. It was difficult to prevail in a case he was presiding over. I walked an employee through some events presented in the file, and without his realizing it, I backed him into stating something that would prove my case. I had one problem, though: as I surveyed the room, I saw that the arbitrator, who used a tape recorder, had dozed off. I knew I was about to make a key point in the case, and right before I lowered the boom on the employee, I banged the table really hard to wake the arbitrator so that he would hear the employee's admission. It worked, and I won the case.

In another case, a window clerk who sold stamps at the main window section at Fort Worth came up a thousand dollars short in her reconciliation and was unable to state that anything unusual had happened to the money. Employees were held strictly accountable for postal stock or monies assigned to them.

It appeared she had stolen the money; however, there was no direct evidence to support that suspicion. The union put her on the stand, and she testified to all sorts of things but could never state clearly what happened to the money. Normally, when an employee is cross-examined, the union would have an opportunity to redirect once the management representative has asked his or her questions. In many cases, the union would be able to refute what was testified by the grievant during management's cross-examination. I knew that the union had not presented any information that exonerated the employee and that the union would pick on anything I opened for discussion, I made the determination to ask the employee one question. I asked her what had happened to the money, and she stated she did not know. That was the first case I ever won with asking only one question.

The next case came after the Postal Service had suffered through the mass shooting that took place in Edmond, Oklahoma, and the shooting of my counterpart in Las Vegas. The case involved a Postal Service investigation in which one of the letter-sorting machines was consistently shutting down, and the cause appeared to be related to employee involvement. The postal inspectors secretly videoed the operation, and the video revealed that an employee was deliberately sabotaging the equipment, causing the machine to shut down and lead to a loss of production time.

The inspection service provided management and Labor Relations a copy of the tape so we could take the appropriate action. I called the clerk craft director, went to the district manager's office, and showed him the tape of the employee sabotaging the machine.

Action was taken to remove the employee, which he appealed to arbitration. During the arbitration, I had plans to call the clerk craft director in to testify since the union was claiming the grievant was blindsided by the removal. When I went out to call the craft director to testify, I warned him to not lie. He went into the arbitration and told the arbitrator that he did not recall my taking him to the district manager's office to show him the tape. Once outside the arbitration room, I called him a liar, and that set him off. He had a relationship with the district manager and reported to him that I had called him a liar. The district manager told me I should not call anyone a liar, and I responded that the manager had lied in arbitration and so he was a liar.

As I was going to the restroom, I passed the union advocate and the employee we had fired in the hallway, and the employee popped off to me. I mistakenly responded and almost got into a confrontation him. Even though the union did what it normally would do—that is, lie—the Postal Service prevailed, and I had another notch on my belt.

Due to threats made to Labor Relations professionals, we had a special buzzer installed in our office that would notify the Postal Inspection Service if it appeared we were under threat. After receiving the arbitration decision, the employee we fired came to the post office to take care of his final business, and we noticed him quickly moving toward the Labor Relations offices. The secretary was just about to press the buzzer when the employee presented a legitimate question. That was a relief.

Speaking of my secretary, she was a force in Labor Relations and my right hand. She was a very kind and thoughtful person, one whom I really appreciated and relied on as a staff member. Her name is Natalie Stevenson. Natalie was a full-figured person, but she did not carry herself as someone who was overweight. I never thought about her weight either. However, one day I made a very bad blunder. A station manager I knew well came to my office to discuss business, and he was also overweight. When he came in, I was busy on the telephone with another manager, and I directed him to wait in the adjacent office. When I finished my conversation, I called out to the manager, "Get your fat ass in here." What happened next truly embarrassed me and taught me a lesson at the same time. Natalie came running into my office with pencil and pad and said, "Did you call me?" I was so embarrassed that all I could do was apologize and assure her that I would never talk to her like that. I explained that I had been talking to the station manager in the other office. As for the station manager, he had a good laugh about the situation, and I am not sure he made the situation any better. Lesson learned.

Many employees created anxious moments for Labor Relations, and I would be remiss if I did not talk about the craziest person to have worked in the Maintenance Department. I first met the guy in 1986, after assuming the Labor Relations representative position. He came to my office and stood in my door while I was responding to a question from a manager. After I hung up the phone, he asked me a question, and I responded. I could not be sure, but he seemed a bit upset by my phone conversation, but he only stated that he did not agree with the response I gave him. I did not know him, and I attempted once again to explain to him the Postal Service's position on his question. He wanted to argue with me, and I had to ask him to leave my office. He refused. I asked him again, and he stated he would not leave and told me to put him out. I got up out of my seat and tried to get by him as he was blocking my door. When I got close to him, he stated, "Why don't you hit me?" I then knew that I was dealing with a pure fool. Finally, I stepped outside my office to get a witness to my instructions to this obvious fool to leave my office. He left before a witness arrived. A day or so later, the Maintenance craft director came to my office and inquired about the incident. Word of his foolishness had evidently gotten around the post office. The craft director informed me that this strange individual was competing against her for the position of Maintenance craft director, and she wanted to make sure the Postal Service was not planning on taking any action against him. If we did, she requested that we allow her to take credit for it. There was no action pending, and I agreed to not pursue any. I said that if she wanted to take credit, she could. Her plan did not work, and the nutcase won the election.

A few years later, the nutcase was being challenged for his craft director position by one of his stewards, and he came to the Personnel office seeking the employee's official personnel folder under the pretense of investigating a grievance. But he was seeking personal information on his political rival.

The competitor came to Human Resources and filed a complaint stating the employee had used personal information out of his personnel file against him. Based on that information, it was determined that the craft director had inappropriately used his position for a personal matter. The Postal Service used that information as a basis for terminating the craft director. He appealed his removal to the Merit System Protection Board and hired a former administrative judge to represent him. I admit we erred in taking the action because we should have known what would happen. The person who brought the violation to our attention was deeply embedded in the union, so we should have known that the union still had influence over him. When we went to the hearing, he softened his story and all but recanted what was reported. Not only did he fail to testify correctly, but the union, as they were known to do, brought in a zinger—that is, their liar. The person the union called to testify was a well-known union arbitration advocate whom I had gone against on many occasions. He came in and testified under oath that I had threatened to fire this person once before; I guess he was alluding to the incident that happened in my office, for which I sought no action, and I never threatened to fire him. However, I had no way of proving that I did not threaten him. The administrative judge presiding basically told me that I was losing the case, so I agreed to return this nutcase to work, with back pay.

This guy had a new lease on life and became a nightmare for Labor Relations. I am not sure if he was trying to punish management and Labor Relations or if he was trying to become a full-time steward, even though there were not enough Maintenance craft employees to justify the time he was using to file grievances. Handling them had evolved into a full-time job. John Merritt handled Maintenance craft grievances, and he would spend endless time trying to reason with this guy. Nothing worked. As an example, occasionally unions would contact Labor Relations and ask us to go through a process to remove backlogged grievances from the arbitration log, where we would "pre-arbs" cases, which meant we would sit down with our union counterpart and try to resolve as many cases as possible to prevent spending the money on arbitration. The process called for compromise on both parties. This nutcase would come to the meeting and ask for the exact same thing he had asked for in the regular grievance procedure. He did not understand what *compromise* meant, and nothing happened.

He continued to file numerous grievances and tied up a lot of John's time. However, thing would change. Not only were we getting sick and tired of him, the leadership in the APWU union was also getting tired of his antics.

However, I had a little fun with him before he was neutered by the union. He was reproducing grievances with the exact same alleged contractual violations, and when he would come upstairs to our offices, he would have a stack of twenty to thirty grievances that he wanted to present. When he met with John, he would set out to process each grievance independently, even though they were identical. He would spend in excess of an hour and sometimes two hours arguing each grievance with John. I told John that he was giving the guy too much credit as he continued trying to reason with an unreasonable person.

When John went on vacation, I assumed his duties in his absence. I scheduled a meeting with the craft director to hear the Maintenance grievances he had appealed to step two. He walked into my office with a stack of grievances, and as he prepared to sit in the seat across from my desk but before his butt hit the chair, I told him to hold it. I am sure he had planned to sit there and go through each grievance individually, tying up my time as he did John's, so I asked him if the grievances he had in his arms were the same ones he had been filing, and he stated that they were. I told him that each grievance was denied and to get his ass out of my office. He did not challenge my instructions this time, and he left without incident. Now that was fun. The union filed grievances all over the United States involving staffing of custodial positions, and they usually prevailed, which had major implications for every post office that had custodial staffing. Based on the major arbitration decision, it was advised that each office meet with the union and negotiate a settlement to lessen the liability.

I gave the assignment to Bill Jackson and had him meet with the new Maintenance craft director in an attempt to settle the cases that would prevent us from having to go to arbitration, which would put us at the mercy of an arbitrator who would be compelled to follow the prior decision, which was call *stare decisis*. Weeks and weeks went by with no movement or compromise. Bill told me the craft director would not budge off a number that was close to what we would be liable to pay if we went to arbitration. I took over the negotiation. I was aware that the craft director had promised the custodians a Christmas present and that he would distribute the money from the settlement to them prior to Christmas. It was now November. I met with him, and we tossed around a few numbers, and he knew that he did not have to budge too far off what the arbitrator would award if the case was pushed to arbitration. He was unaware of the leverage I had, though, and that I knew about his promise to the custodians. I knew he wanted to get the case settled before Christmas to keep his promise, so I had a little fun with him. I pulled my offer off the table and told him that I would see him in arbitration. I was aware that the case would have to be scheduled and would not be heard for approximately six months. The APWU president was in the meeting, and he called the craft director outside to discuss my previous settlement offer. The craft director was over a barrel, and he needed to settle to keep his promise. I sweetened the pot a little bit, and we settled.

In another negotiation period with the NALC Union pertaining to a national violation of the contract where postal managers arbitrarily changed the meaning of the contract, I was in charge of the negotiation, along with my good friend James Conley, who was an area manager for Customer Services. We were instructed to settle the local grievances, and funds were later set aside to pay the union for the violations. I was not aware of the reserved money, and when we met with the union, we agreed to settle the grievances by agreeing to honor the language of the Carrier Handbook and the contract. After we had verbal settlement, one of the stewards raised the issue of compensation for every carrier in the city since it was a citywide violation. I agreed we should compensate individual carriers, and then I told the steward that I believed the supervisors should be compensated as well because they had been caught in the middle of a higher-manager decision. Then I told the room full of NALC officers and stewards that, since the issue was a national issue, we should agree to pay every letter carrier and every supervisor in the United States, and after doing that, we would just close up the damn place because we would be broke. It got awfully quiet in the room, and the issue was not discussed further. We signed the agreement without any compensation. I later found out that headquarters had set aside funds to pay for the grievances; however, it was to late for the local union because they had signed on the dotted line. Sorry.

I mentioned earlier that John Merritt was a good addition to our Labor Relations staff, but I did not always feel that way. I thought he was too nice a guy to deal with the ugliness of Labor Relations. When he met with union officials, he would always appeal to their better nature, and that was not usually my way. I was more confrontational. John dealt with another sorry person who tried to function as a union steward and who held a black belt in karate, as I was told. When the provisions of the Family Medical Leave Act were implemented, the steward bragged that we could not take an action against him for using sick-leave benefits. John did the best that he could in trying to work with him, but I always tried to pull his chain when I could. This steward was also one the union would bring into arbitration solely to lie. Strangely enough, the district manager liked this guy, and I was not sure why; in addition, he once asked me to detail this guy to Labor Relations. I almost lost it and almost became disrespectful, but I modified my objection to be more respectful.

I had some interesting experiences with the Postal Inspection Service long before I developed a great relationship with them. One day an inspector came to my office and asked me about Bill Jackson, who drove to work in a top-of-the-line Mercedes and parked it where it was visible from the third floor, where the inspectors were domiciled. He wanted to know how Bill was driving a Mercedes to work on a postal salary. I knew it was none of his business, and as far as I was concerned, it was a racist question. I did not make it any better by embellishing a little. For background information, Bill was a retired army major, and his wife was a schoolteacher. I had just read a newspaper article about Oliver North's retirement pay, which was not too shabby. So I said to the inspector, "You don't know about Bill. He is a retired army lieutenant colonel, and his wife is a high school principal. He has more money than he knows what to do with it." Needless to say, the inspector left my office with a strange look on his face.

In another case, the inspection service called me on the carpet because I had failed to take an action they recommended. For the record, it was my job to determine whether there was enough evidence to take corrective action against an employee. The case involved an employee who claimed he was injured when he fell through a rotten front porch, but the inspection service felt the employee had deliberately walked onto the rotten boards to claim an injury. I went to the residence, which was in a small city south of Fort Worth, to assess the condition of the porch. However, it had been repaired, so it was difficult for me to even see where the damage and repair had been. I disagreed with a request for discipline that was being pushed by the inspection service through the employee's supervisor, who also did not believe discipline was appropriate. I did not think anything further about my decision until, about a month later, I was called to the district manager's office. He told me that there was an inquiry from the Postal Inspection Service, Southern Region headquarters, about my failure to take action. I had to write a report justifying my decision, and that was the end of it.

The Postal Service put an emphasis on programs to enhance opportunities for minorities in the workplace. I was not aware of it at the time, but some Hispanic employees resented me. Apparently, it had begun when I was selected over Oscar Ochoa for the Labor Relations representative position. I heard a few behind-the-scenes comments, but I did not think much about them. I felt that the Hispanics who were making the comments did not know my background or maybe just believed that Oscar should have gotten the position based on his background as clerk craft director and his year or so working as a Labor Relations assistant.

After I selected Oscar for a permanent position in Labor Relations, I thought we had developed a very good working relationship in that few problems or concerns surfaced. However, problems began to come up. Some Labor Relations officials liked to handle step-two grievances that are appealed to arbitration, especially contract grievances. One of the first things that hinted Oscar was unhappy with me was when he came to my office and told me that he did not think we could prevail in an arbitration that appeared to be a grievance I had handled or made a decision on at step two. This was the first time any Labor Relations representative had taken such a step. It was not unusual to settle a grievance if we were able to get something of value out of the settlement. Oscar had indicated to me that the case was a loser and we could not get anything out of it. But he had come to me on the day the case was scheduled, which ticked me off. I took the case, presented it in arbitration, and prevailed. I believe he was a little embarrassed, but he did not say anything else to me.

We were having problems in the Finance Unit, where one female supervisor had a history of what looked like discrimination against minorities. Oscar had been prepping a young Hispanic woman in filing an EEO complaint against the supervisor. I noticed him in the breakroom speaking to the young lady, and I thought it was odd because I knew she had filed an EEO. Labor professionals would usually keep their distance from someone in litigation against the Postal Service because it was Labor Relations' mandate to represent the Postal Service in those forums. As a result, I started wondering about whether Oscar's allegiance was to the Hispanic organization or the Postal Service.

I confronted him one morning and asked him if he was advising the young lady in her complaint against the Postal Service. I personally believe the Hispanic employees felt somewhat emboldened because we were under the management of our second Hispanic district manager. I was aware that Oscar had developed a relationship with the district manager, so I told him that if he felt the young lady had a legitimate complaint and if the evidence supported that she had been discriminated against, then he should go to the district manager and tell him we needed to resolve the case. The young lady had requested a large monetary settlement, and I knew that the district manager would not agree to the settlement request. So did Oscar.

The conversation got heated to the point that he let it all out. He told me that I favored settling cases involving Black employee and not Hispanics. He reminded me of two identical issues involving a Black and a Hispanic employee who filed EEO complaints against the female supervisor over the Finance section who was still having problems. Oscar stated that I had resolved the case involving the Black employee but failed to resolve the case involving the Hispanic employee. He really believed I had personally discriminated against the Hispanic employee. What Oscar did not know was that I had not resolved the case involving the Black employee.

In the EEO hearing process, the administrative judge assigned to hear the case would also hold a prehearing conference in which the judge would normally browbeat the management representative into resolving the case, especially if it appeared discrimination had taken place. I did not agree to resolve the case, and the administrative judge did everything she could to persuade me. The administrative judge just happened to be

Black, and as we were walking out of the hearing room, she noticed Willie Hathman. She asked me if he was the postmaster, and I said he was. She walked up to him and told him that we were going to lose that case if we went to hearing. Willie told me to resolve the case. After drawing up the language, I presented it to him, he agreed with the language, and the case was resolved, with the Black employee receiving an upgrade in his position in Finance. To make matters worse, I spoke with Willie and the director of Finance to inform them that the female supervisor in Finance was discriminating against her employees and that she had failed to implement the agreed-upon settlement. The Finance manager did not like the idea that his unit was being accused of discrimination and then being forced to do something based on a claim of discrimination. Like most managers, he was protective of his territory. Willie basically had to instruct him to implement the agreement. He and I had a few words before Willie intervened, stopping me from saying too much. I knew I had screwed up because, shortly after returning to my office, I received a call from Willie, who asked me to come to his office. I knew I was in trouble. Willie had a unique way of letting people know they had messed up. He told me that I just might have made a powerful enemy. He said that, someday I might be interviewing for a higher-level position, and I just might have to interview with this manager. His message hit home.

A few months later I got the second case involving Finance. This time, a Hispanic employee had almost the same claim of discrimination against the female supervisor. I knew I was not in a position to even consider trying to resolve the case. Strangely, the case was arbitrated before a Hispanic female administrative judge, and yes, she ruled in favor of the employee. As stated earlier, Oscar thought I treated the Black and Hispanic employees in disparate ways, which was not true.

The conversation that Oscar and I had in my office involving the female Hispanic employee he was trying to help resulted in a full-fledged blow-up between us that actually ended his tenure in Labor Relations. He requested an assignment as a level 18 postmaster. He even requested that the district manager allow him to keep his level 19 position, but the manager did not agree.

I also learned through a document produced by a Hispanic organization that the feeling was that Black employees had received preferential treatment and more higher-level promotions than Hispanic employees. Strangely enough, the document indicated the organization was targeting Black managers and not White managers, who held most of the higher-level positions. I never understood their logic, but it did explain to me why some Hispanics in the office resented me and other Black managers.

Finally, I got a legitimate threat on my life from an employee who appeared on The Jerry Springer Show complaining about how bad it was to work for the Postal Service. The employee would come to the post office dressed in bulky clothes and sometimes carrying a backpack. Even though this was prior to the frequent bomb threats we have received, I did not take any chances. One time, he came onto the property, and I had to instruct him to stay off Postal Service property. A postal inspector called me and said this employee was seeing a psychiatrist. During a recent session, he told the psychiatrist of some postal employees he would like to kill, and I was near the top of the list. I was told to keep a lookout for him and informed about the make of his car.

One thing that I did as a Labor Relations representative and manager was develop an excellent working relationship with the local APWU president. He was kind of fun to hang out with, so I would go over to his office, drink his liquor, and talk ugly to him. He loved it and always invited me over for their annual Christmas party. While I was attending the last Christmas party before retiring, sitting in his office drinking his bourbon, the employee who had threatened to kill me came to the party. I did not initially see him, and he did not know I was there; however, when I started moving around, he saw me. He rushed outside, went to his car, and sped off. The union president advised me to leave in fear the employee would come back with a weapon. I left as advised. I do not know whether he returned, but I did not hear anything else about this strange person.

As I was winding down my postal career, I was able to take a few trips that I found enjoyable. My boss was unable to attend a managers' meeting in San Antonio, so I went in his stead. I finally saw how the managers were treated in relation to the rest of us. After our meeting, the group went to a famous restaurant in the Market Street area. While sitting in our private room having margaritas, the person in charge told us that the meal and the drinks were on the Postal Service, and we could order anything we wanted off the menu. Well, when you are not used to getting anything, you tend to overdo it. I had five or six margaritas and ordered a steak with my Mexican meal. Great steak and a great time. After dinner, we went back to our hotel, which was located downtown and near a bar that had what was credited as the longest bar in Texas. As I walked down the street from the hotel, I noticed several postal employees in the bar, and they beckoned for me to come in. They were doing tequila shots and ordered me one, which led to six or seven. Strangely enough, I was still standing when everybody decided to leave. The group paid the bar tab, and all I had was a nice buzz. I am not sure to this day why that is. It was a great introduction to how managers lived.

On another trip, my boss and I traveled to New York to attend a major Postal Service seminar being held at a high-end hotel in Manhattan, not too far from Times Square. We decided to bring along our spouses, which offered us an opportunity to show our wives a good time. Each evening after attending the seminar, we would explore the city. We even had a steak dinner at a restaurant named Broadway Joes.

On the last day of the seminar, we were released early and had most of the day to ourselves before our flight back to Texas. My wife and I wanted to go up to Harlem. I told Joe Bob about our plans, and since his wife was going up to Martha's Vineyard to visit a relative, he said he wanted to tag along.

My wife had done some shopping and had a Saks Fifth Avenue bag with a few items in it, and as we got off the subway in Harlem, a homeless person lying on the sidewalk muttered, "Saks Fifth Avenue." This scared my wife, and she felt she should not have carried that bag. I had been to Harlem before and was not concerned for our safety. However, as we were walking to the Apollo Theater, we saw a Black policeman who had to have been at least six foot five and three hundred pounds. I asked him jokingly if one had to be that big to be a cop in Harlem, and he responded, "No, but it helps." He had a great attitude and was not offended by my stupid question.

We were able to take a tour through the Apollo Theater and saw the walk of fame, where there was a collage of entertainers who had performed at the Apollo over the many years of its existence. It was a great tour. We left the Apollo and went up to Sylvia's Restaurant, soul-food heaven. I do not know if Job

Bob had ever eaten at a soul-food restaurant, but I know he had not been to Sylvia's. After the waitress passed out the menus, I immediately saw what I would order—something I had been introduced to years earlier by my aunt Ethel and a dish I often indulged in when I was traveling to Houston as an ad-hoc EEO investigator at a place called This Is It. The dish was oxtails. To my surprise, Joe Bob ordered the same thing. I am not sure he really wanted oxtails; he was just trusting I had made a good selection. I did not leave anything on my plate, but Joe Bob did not eat all his. I am not sure he enjoyed the dish as I did.

After returning to Fort Worth, not many noteworthy events occurred other than signing off on a few grievances. The Postal Service was liable for hundreds of thousands of dollars, and I had to put my name on the agreements. It really made me sick, mainly because management had been warned that their decisions violated the agreement but decided to take an untenable position that cost the Postal Service dearly. The whole situation was very stressful to me, and as I sat there thinking, it dawned on me that I had turned fifty-five in October. We were now in early November, and I was eligible to retire anytime I wanted. I decided that I had had enough and it was time to retire. I informed Joe Bob of my decision, and he asked me to hang around for one more year just to wind down. I told him that I had been winding down over the previous year.

For a poor kid from the projects of east Fort Worth, I achieved things beyond my wildest dreams and had a great postal career. Going postal was well worth the ride.